KARLO MILA

First published in 2020 by Huia Publishers
39 Pipitea Street, PO Box 12-280
Wellington, Aotearoa New Zealand
www.huia.co.nz

Reprinted in 2021

ISBN 978-1-77550-400-9 (Paperback)
ISBN 978-1-77550-635-5 (Hardback)

Text copyright © Karlo Mila 2020

Illustrations and graphics copyright:
Illustration cover photo © Karlo Mila
Cover illustrated elements © Isobel Joy Te Aho-White
Carving image on dedication page © Papa Sean Bennett-Ogden
Page 10 © Naomi Maraea
Pages 50 & 68 © Delicia Sampero
Pages 70–71, 74 & 78 © Meleanna Meyer

This book is copyright. Apart from fair dealing for the purpose of private study, research, criticism or review, as permitted under the Copyright Act, no part may be reproduced by any process without the prior permission of the publisher.

A catalogue record for this book is available from the
National Library of New Zealand.

For Papa Sean

who gave me the language
to describe another world

Contents

Your People Will Gather around You: Love after Love   4

E Ngā Mate, Haere, Haere, Haere
Malaga: The Journey   8
Oceania   11
For Teresia Teaiwa   14
Bottled Ocean   17
A Conversation with Hone Tuwhare   20
Letter to J C Sturm   22

This Is How We Make a World
Tagaloa: The Order of Things   30
In the Beginning   34
Papatūānuku   37
Te Awa: Love Song for Manawatū   41
Matau Mana Moana   44
Mana   46
Ngatu   48

The Good Wife's Prayer
Lonely   52
Readjusting Great Expectations   54
A Woman Scorned   55
The Unfaithful Heart of Her Quiet   57
Bruise   58
Terms of a Treaty   59
Enter Hot Man at an International Conference   61
Itinerary of Infidelity   62
summer, bed, awake, alone,   63
Let Me Tell You What I Remember   64
Whiro   65
Love Isn't   67
The Good Wife's Prayer   68

Hawai'i Found

What the Students Said: O'ahu 313	72
Tūtū Pele Intervenes	73
Our Generation: 'Āina Aloha	74
Intergenerational Healing: Lessons from Hawai'i	78
Anchoring the Cry from Within	80
Kūkaniloko	84

Demigods in Archetype City

Shark	88
Hina: Advice Column across the Ages	90
The Tale of Hina and Sinilau	92
Hina and Her Pool	94
Rupe/Lupe	95
What Trees Will Say	96

One Last Lifetime

Dry-docked	100
Wedding River Song	104
Is That a Sex Poem?	107
Go-betweens	109
Bloodshed	111
Carved on a Pou	114
You've written a lot of poems, he said	116
Odyssey in Black Sand	118
How to Break a Curse	124

Telling the Other Side of the Story

After Reading *Ancestry*	132
Son, for the Return Home	133
We Find Ourselves Statistics	136
Finding Our Way	138
Our Fears	141
Moemoeā	142
A Tongan Reflection on Tino Rangatiratanga	150

Tūhoe Boys	152
For Tamir, with Love from Aotearoa	155
Now THIS is Reverse Racism	159
For All My Sisters	164

Lost and Found

The Sounds of *Princess Ashika*	174
Spirited Leadership	177
Lost and Found	181
Poem for the Commonwealth, 2018	185
Kapihe's Prophesy	189
Matariki: A Call to Kāinga	192

The Art of Walking in Dark Light

Te Korekore	198
Te Pō: The Dark Ages	200
Te Ao Mārama: The World of Light	201
Unbecoming	202
The Art of Walking in Dark Light	205
Goddess Muscle Meditation	207

Acknowledgements	214

YOUR PEOPLE WILL GATHER AROUND YOU: LOVE AFTER LOVE

Your people
will gather around you.

Your family
who prepared
a place for you,
in a lineage
that connects you
all the way back
to the beginning.

A family
that dreamed you
possible.

It is their
soft singing,
cellular love songs,
the chanting lyric of bloodlines,
accompanying you
all the way
through the lonely.

The benefactors of your bones,
blood, and body.
Each is a love letter
folded in your DNA sequence.
With double-helix tongues
they whisper you
into your dreams.
Why you are here.
What you are meant to do.
Hoping you have ears
in your waking life
and eyes to see.

They call you to transform
the weft and warp
of what has been
woven before you.

To bring it back
into balance.

It is their magnetic pull
of molecule
that gathers all that is lost
and redirects your return
to centre.

Reorients you
to radiant nucleus.

Re-sourced.

So you can widen your circles
of compassion; travel beyond
your own limits, beyond almost
what you can bear.
Accompanied all the way.

Yes, this is the large, large,
ever-expanding loving
of everything
that has been the making of us.
Knowing itself
through you
and evolving.

Yes, your people
will hold fast within you.
In the marrow of your bones,
waiting to be known.
Travelling with you
along the soft breathing
curves of an infinite circle
that has no circumference,
and whose centre
is everywhere.

Ever so slowly,
all your people will gather around you,
the ones you realise, when you look in their eyes,
that you've known for a life cycle, or two,
who not only help you on your journey
to find home,
but who make it home,
this strange lonely journey,
who make it home as you travel it.

And then time will come
with great knowing,
when you will remember yourself
back to yourself.

Returning
to a memory
of wholeness.

E NGĀ MATE,

HAERE, HAERE, HAERE

MALAGA: THE JOURNEY

(FOR ALICE SUISANA HUNT)

It is a spindrift
that rises from the body.
Our final exhale
beyond the breath,
where we give ourselves up
in completion
to life.

Where everything that you are
leaves behind
everything that you were.

Departing
that faithful friend
of the body.
Its soft limbs.
Its forgiving flesh.
Muscles, skin, sinews –
all that held you together –
so gently,
for so long.
A song
of water, blood,
breath and bone.

We acknowledge all
that you have left behind.

All that you have given.
And what a life you have seen,
and what a life you have been
and how we have loved you.

We stay here,
with that precious vessel
that carried you
through this life,
but cannot carry you
into the next.

And may we who loved you,
holding the song, blood and bone vessel
    of your being,
may we carry the meaning
of your life forward
into the world of light,
so that it will reach
those who come after.

He waka herehere ngā waka.

The vessel that binds us
to the great moving fleet.

We know that it's your time to depart,
to embark on an ancient route of return,

along the terrestrial contours of this land
that has birthed and fed you,
this land on which we stand,
towards a celestial flight path
beyond the wingspan of birds,
into the stars,
towards the warmer weather of our dreams,
towards islands we have held gently in our
    memories,
where we once belonged.

At Te Rerenga Wairua,
where two oceans meet,
a pōhutukawa tree still holds,
waiting for you
with a fragrant, green-leaved,
red-crowned,
farewell.

The whole earth heaves
a sigh of release.
And from here,
wreathed in red and green,
you will bid us farewell
and begin to travel the ocean roads.
The sea path traced by star walkers,
past Tongatapu, to 'Uvea and Futuna,
where with the splitting of rocks, it all began.

You will enter the deep, blue channels
of ocean and night
and move between worlds

of underwater darkness and celestial light.
You will take flight.

Until you reach Savai'i
and follow the black lava fields
towards the last rites.

Here, you will be cleansed
in the waters of Falealupo.
The final farewell at the seashore.
It is here we face that truth,
that you are westward-bound.
Ia Manuia Lou Malaga.
Blessed be your journey.
Follow the shining trail
of the setting sun
towards the great mystery
beyond all of our knowing.
We must trust then,
in all we cannot understand,
and like the land,
heave a heavy sigh of release.

O le mavaega nai le tai e fetaia'i i i'u o gafa.

The farewell at the seashore,
with the promise
to meet again in the children.

OCEANIA
(FOR EPELI HAU'OFA)

Some days
I've been
on dry land
for too long

    my ache
    for ocean
    so great
    my eyes weep
    waves

        my mouth
        mudflats
        popping with
        groping breath
        of crabs

            my throat
            an estuary
            salt crystallising
            on the tip of my tongue

                my veins
                become
                rivers that flow
                straight out to sea

I call on the memory of water
and

    I
    am
    starfish
    in sea

        buoyed by
        lung balloons
        and floating fat

            I know the ocean
            she loves me

                her continuous blue body
                holding even
                my weight

                    flat on my back
                    I feel her

                        outstretched palms
                        legs wide open

                            a star in worship
                            a meditation as old as the tide

my arms, anemones
belly and breasts, sea jellies
Achilles fins, I become
free-swimming medusa

    my hands touching
    her blue curves

        fingers tipping
        spindrift

            a star in worship
            a wafer in her mouth
            a five-pointed offering

                she swirls
                counter-clockwise
                beneath me,
                all goddess
                all muscle, energy
                power, pulse

                    oh, the simple faith
                    of the floating

                        letting go
                        in order to be held
                        by the body water of the world

                            some days
                            this love
                            is all I need

FOR TERESIA TEAIWA

I am going to light a candle for you
e hoa, although at our age
candles should be for lovers
and shy bodies ushering in
trust,
or for mindfulness
at the end of a long
short-wick
of a working day.

Not for this.

He tangi oiaue.

I will light this candle.
The spendy kind,
cradled in glass,
that burns for days
smelling of coconut and vanilla
and I will say prayers for you
even though my prayers
are like bad poems
and are often wordless.

I hope,
at the least,
you will feel the
long-burning
flame of my intent,
warming the space
between us.

You are the first of us
'young ones' –

the OG feminist:
Dr Dusky Maiden,
who famously
cried salt-tears
and sweat ocean,
creating a wake
wide enough
for so many of us
who followed.

In the deep multicolour
of your wide, wonderful wake
I am thinking of a word: Huliau,
described to me once
by a Tongan artist,
but no Google search
reveals its meaning.

And as you well know,
the stuff really worth knowing
isn't found on Google.
Although I see in Hawaiian,
huliau means climate
and sister –
climate changer
feels right to me.

We felt you
change
the climate Tere.
Daughter of Oceania,
ambiguously native,
kin somehow
to all of us.

(Even us polys,
while calling us out,
our volume,
and our
repetitive
raw fish.)

You are,
Maraea nailed it,
'kaupapa as' –
unafraid,
yet overburdened
with community service,
with marking
and mentoring
and doing all of this
and all of that,
with so much
determination
and good grace
it escalates
around you.
Contagious.

Although I for one
wish you had more time
to write poetry
and just sit, very quietly,
wherever you liked.

You are the reason
I sat with coconut cream
in my wild hair
on a wilder beach

in west Auckland,
with other curly girls
in a salt pool
in dark black sand.

You told me via story
that a tatau should never
point to your sex, giggling,
pointing to your paradox.
We were standing, at the time,
next to a replica moai,
but still, it was on a beach –
nobody can laugh at
that southern-most water
too cold to swim in.
And in Wellington,
in a sea of Palangis,
in the windy, wide-eyed dry,
I was thirsty for your stories
of tatau and French Polynesian authors
and an Oceania
more expansive than mine.

Shy admission: more than once
I caught my breath
with how much
there was to admire.
Diplomat: representing us overseas with your
    not-missing-a-beat articulate.
Truth teller: revealing and peeling off
    your skin
in front of students unaccustomed
to real,
in school assemblies
when in uniform.

Activist: in front of everyone
that little bit braver
than the rest of us.

You are
a voice,
a song,
a poem,
an essay,
a direct quote,
a protest sign,
a presence.

Beloved.

You are
my prayer.

BOTTLED OCEAN

(FOR JIM VIVIEAERE)

i)
We shared a beer once.
A quiet conversation
that quickly moved
to what lurks beneath.

You showed me your work:
dark purples, subterranean colours,
images like bite marks into
the deep flesh of memory.

You-made-it-so-beautiful
Bat-winged boy remembering
i-felt-it-so-painful

but

you-held-it-so-lightly

such gentle eyes

the way
one
might bottle
a moving ocean

changing
forever
what is seen
behind the glass.

ii)
Yes,
that exhibition
made it all the way to my hometown,
Palmerston North,
right on time.

Flooding the old, tired,
savage story of us.

Blotting and plotting
lucid watermarks,
washing up another vision entirely.

You were always at the forefront
of the wave.

Even in the unkind infrastructure
    of cities –
betrayals of bureaucracies, blood,
    flesh, and bone –
where soft, brown-eyed boys
are broken
and split open,
betrayed –
in windowless rooms
where tenderness
is turned
in
on
itself,
and will never
return.

boys2men

You found
the whakapapa trail
back to the
open-harboured arms
of unconditional ocean,
ever-present,
where all lost boys
can be both lost
and loved,
with warm waves
promising distant shores
beyond the blue,
where we might be received
by holy women,
fragrant with flowers,
welcoming us home.

All of this dream,
you bottled it.

With a fine eye for
beautiful blemish,
the alchemy
of soft anxieties,
the luminosity
of dark depressions.

Juxtapositions of
plastic and pearl
ancient and fresh

real and surreal
loss and light
gift and grief.

Finely shaped,
carefully thought,
gently wrought.

Installations of
Urbanesia:
incisions,
bite-marks,
we slash and cut,
stitch and sew,
bind and lash.

On urban drift
wood, we pull
out our blades
and carve
new pou,
muttering karakia
for these times,
black inking
our steps.

We mark
our stories
in flesh.
We dare
to be here.

Carve
our own
freshwater faces.
We take our places,
among the ancestral real.
We sit among
the all-seeing eyes.

E pou,
You are an ancestor at the apex
of this new meeting house,
where our artists gather
to determine our fate.

A CONVERSATION WITH HONE TUWHARE

Hone,

I can afford to buy-you-by-the-book
these days
instead of take you out.

Small holes in
my pockets.
Middleclassy.

It can put an honest man off.

You boilermaker,
fabricating lyrical weld
from blast furnace
of sun,
slowed,
stopped and
set
on white horizon
of page.

Flames on your fingers, Māui,
wrestling words and worlds.

Nothing ordinary about it.

Like that alchemical asshole
crawling into places he shouldn't go:
repipe, retube, repair.

Hine-nui-te-pō
has had her way with you –
but still
you speak
on page –
a fantail laughing.

Trickster.

You and I both know,
the ones who break the rules
get the chicks.

You and I both know
how after a while
we stop dedicating poems to our
loves, crushes or would-be-loves.
There are too many
who could drape those
fancy, flimsy stanzas
against their ribs;
stretch them to fit.
OSFA.

I think of your lips
slurping the genitalia
of kaimoana.

Endless odes to small holes.

When my memory
of the sound of you
is translated,
it tastes like
fish.

LETTER TO J C STURM

Dear Jacquie,

I have repeatedly tried to write the poem
'Dear Jim'. And failed.
May I call you Te Kare?
I looked it up on the online dictionary:
1. Kare (*noun*) dear friend.
2. Kare (*verb*) to long for, desire ardently, to whip.
3. Kare (*noun*) ripple, surface of the sea.

Te Kare, will you be my friend?
Can I tell you my story?
I can't write anything for him.

My mother and I,
we went to Hiruharama, Jerusalem
after Hine-nui-te-pō
visited us.

Fantails were flapping indoors
alarm birds winging,
alarm birds ringing.
Our matriarch lay dead.

My grandmother
moved between worlds.
I am still in the soft, dark feathers
of Hine-nui-te-pō.

I am not ready to come back.

Wreathed with grief,
fragile with fresh mourning,
I read Baxter's letters,
tasked with writing back.
So many pages. All his words.
His too-many words,
so many written for other women.
He grew smaller
and smaller with every page.
His over-published words,
until I had nothing left to say to him.

But moving under all that surface skimming
was you. Rippling beneath
every page, Te Kare,
His longing, the whiplash,
the reliable tide.
All depth to his shallows.

I sought out his biggest idea.
Heaving in your direction.
My mother and I took
the winding roads
to Whanganui
in search of Jerusalem,
to see if his vision
had borne fruit.

The world is full of men with visions.

We stopped at the museum,
met the hei tiki
of Tahupōtiki Wiremu Rātana
around the neck
of a green-eyed woman.
Nosy, she said, his taonga was nosy,
as I told her our business.

And Jacquie, to be honest,
I was carrying my own ache.
Not just the death of my matriarch,
but an old-fashioned
broken heart.

He is the river.
And the river is him.

I am waewae tapu here.
To show our respect,
we pulled over and parked.
I took off my jandals,
did a small mihi
to a great awa.

I watched the alchemy of sunlight
transform liquid mud
into slow-moving molten.
Gold is the only colour
you could call it. Te Kare.
It's a cliché, and neither you
nor I are fans of those,
but I have the photos to prove it.

Te Awa Tupua,
ancient highway
of the human and not-quite human,
all sorts of things travelling
in a full-veined,
gold-blooded
river-road.
Motorway
of a waka-nation.

On the winding land road,
we passed through London –
Rānana, Athens – Ātene,
Corinth – Koriniti,
unexpected reincarnations
of faraway places.
Settled uncomfortably
on the hips of the old awa,
like new ideas that haven't really
been thought through.

We finally found Jerusalem.
His big idea.
The one he swore might reunite you.

He hoped
the church would one day
have a carved
whare-whakairo face.
But I am sad to report Jacquie,
although it may not surprise you,
the kōwhaiwhai patterns
were made out of cardboard.

The church was an empty meeting house.

We looked for Jim. There was no trace.
The convent was closed.
He was
a few lines
in a paper pamphlet.

We asked the woman at the shops
about his grave.
'On private property,'
we were told,
as she reached for iceblocks
in the freezer.
I could tell by the tightness on her face
that we were hōhā.

And that vision he'd had
of te ao Māori and te ao Pākehā,
of a movement, of a meeting place,
so public, so full of people,
an open-hearted marae,
felt so buried
behind a gated grave
on private land,
attracting unwanted tourists
we didn't want to be.

My mate told me,
after reading this poem.
It's not private land.
It's Māori land.
It's whānau land.
Te whenua o Patiarero.
It has always been.

And yes, James, you were a flick of a flame.
Jerusalem, one single smouldering century,
in the continuous fires of ahi kā.

You would have known this Jacquie,
more than he could have ever understood.

He prophesied
he'd become an old kūmara
thrown rightly over the fence.

I know you were buried by your grandmother,
near your maunga Taranaki,
at your mother's feet.
The one who was taken from you
a few weeks after your birth,
not far from the green sea.

This is happy ending
enough for me.

James also prophesied
that he would be broken,
which has also happened.
'James K. Baxter the rapist'
the headline reads,
unearthed
all these years later.

It is tempting Jacquie,
to crucify him on the cross.
But it strikes me
that he was already
so willingly there.
Hanging his head in shame.
I have no taste for it.

That self-loathing cycle:
abstinence, sin, repent, repeat.
I can understand how you might
have had no time for that.

I watch the Catholic church
keep on forgiving itself
for unforgivable crimes.
Here is what I can tell you, Te Kare.
Here's the good news.
James predicted
that a time would come
when the tree would move
against the church.
And yes, the time is coming.

We are remembering
Tāne Māhuta,
a forest of uplifted ancestors,
the great living pou
of uncarved faces.
We are remembering
all the atua:
earth, sea, skies, trees.
They hold up
the balance
of a changing
climate.

The time is coming.
A tipping point,
where we will kneel
at the knees of kauri
and beg for forgiveness.

Te Kare,
we will enter
the forest,
Place our offerings
on the altars of ancient rocks.
Meet with great reverence
the holiness of all fresh water.

This is the great remembering.

Speaking of men with visions,
on the day I started writing this poem,
Rua Kenana was pardoned.
James, the Pākehā face
is not seen as so smooth these days
and not so blind.
Today, we know the Māori face cannot
be torn and bloody
without the blood being
on someone's hands.

Rua Kenana was pardoned today.
And something deeply wounded
was touched.
A son made to lie face down in the dirt
and wait to be shot from behind.
The other already dead.

It was remembered as an injustice
by those who benefit
when we forget.

Something stirred, Te Kare,
that would have given you faith,
I believe, in a future forward.

Behind every great prophet
is often a woman left
holding a baby.

All that need,
he had
to be
the seed.

But
instead,
you nurtured
the seed
of flesh and blood.
Gave up on your writing
to look after your moko.

These are the seeds that bear fruit.

I know Hēmi wanted to be a
nobody and a door.
I've come to understand
that to stand and know your place
on indigenous land,
you can't choose the luxury
of
nobody.

Hēmi wanted to be nobody
and a door
in the windowless
room of the dark night.

This is where we meet.
He and I.
I know the windowless room
of the dark night.

And here
is where my hypocrisy is laid bare.
I was standing in that river.
A flicker. A fast-burning flame.

I was standing knee-deep
in grief in Pipiriki,
in that river, repenting.
Asking to please, please,
let me be washed clean.

Let all the unwanted leave.

Words well-known to those of us,
who walk in the windowless
room of the dark night.

But I also know dear Jacquie,
as do you,
that you
cannot desire to
be the door
if you ever
want
to step through it.

THIS IS HOW WE MAKE A WORLD

TAGALOA:
THE ORDER
OF THINGS

Alone

in the
vānimonimo

– vast
illimitable
expansive
space –

alone.

Tangaloa-faʻa-tutupu-nuʻu

a rock

split by strong comet hands,

a big bang

split into named rocks:
Tagaloa-faʻa-tutupu-nuʻu
Papa-taʻoto; Papa-sosolo; Papa-lau-aʻau;
Papa-ʻano-ʻano; Papa-ʻele; Papa-tu;
Papa-ʻamu-ʻamu and
his children –

the oldest sedimentary surfaces.

With meteorite might
split it open to the right.

Earth

– that cooled
rocky crust
became
the parent
of all things
blessed
with vapour.

Then the sea came

and then the
fresh water

and sky.

Each had
offspring:

primordial
chemicals
ancestral
atoms of mutual
attraction

male and female
paired

elements
gravitating
towards
each other

copulating
bifurcating
replicating

molecular
lovemaking.

Immensity
(male)
and space
(female)
were attracted
to each other.

Massive crush
of clouds,
dust and gas –
interstellar sex

procreating
night and day.

Night and day
were attracted
to each other.

Coupled
copulated

procreating
the eye of the sky –
the sun.

Then the moon
and their siblings –
the stars.

A series
of amino-acidic
attractions,

protein reactions,
elements birthing
in a stellar nursery.

Eventually
the youngest,

the islands,
were birthed.

Plants paved the way
for all other forms of life.
Yams and arrowroot
among the elder siblings.
Finally
what was called
the peopling-vine.

Microscopic worms
began to burrow.

A multitude
of worms,
multicellular,

eventually
nerves, vertebrate,
muscle structure.
Much later:
head, faces, hands,
finally distinguishable
as organisms
that evolved
eventually
into us.

At the end of
these ongoing
expressions
of love
and productive

relationships
of mutual attraction,
all life flourished.

An evolutionary
eco-diversity.

A genealogical order.
A world of relatives.

An interconnected
DNA sequence.

A phylogenetic
family tree.

We are
the younger siblings
subordinate to all that
preceded us.

Our role is to serve
and respect our elders.

We are a part of, not apart,
a family of relatives.

All of us
returning
to common
ancestor.
Stardust
still shining
in our bones.

IN THE BEGINNING
(FOR NANA)

In the beginning
was the word:
a breath
given sound;
an arch of throat;
a musical note;
a noise
moving its way
into meaning;
an intention fluted up
from the heart,
through the windpipe,
throated into utterance –
the relief of release.

In the beginning
was the word:
a vibration; a hum;
a whistle that flew like a bird
out of the mouth of a God,
like a lyrical hiss from a volcano,
that landed, rested, nested,
that lava reaching
the ear of the universe,
interrupting the heavy,
hushed tones of void,
reverberating its way
into not-yet-galaxy;
a meteor of sound
  e x p l o d e d
into stars, gasses, echo,
vibration, frequency,
spinning bits of broken planets,
gravity heaving it all in,
gathered with magnetic hands
and the soft words were:
'let there be light,'
and so it was –
stellar and solar.

In the beginning
was the word.
There was no return
to the paradise
of the silent, wide-eyed
innocence of fish,
of the synchrony
of animal gesturing
the beating of the chest of the ape.
Once the upright
word was uttered,
two-legged mother sounds
were muttered
to comfort the cry of newborns
communicating in primal scream –
once, *Mum, mum, mum* meant 'her'
and *Da, da, Dad* meant 'him',
and we recognised
the warm hitherto of come
and the ambiguous directive of go,
the multiflora ways of saying hello,
the farewell of goodbye,
fragrant and painful in any language.
Then began the business of naming,
knowing, explaining,
relating, communicating, creating.

And then in-between us
was the word,
like birds flying out of our mouths,
reaching, resting
in the other,
holding the wings of each other
gently, nesting.

We become such small gods,
creating our world around us,
giving meaning, tone,
shape, nuance, name,
following the chain letters of narrative,
and we find ourselves in story,
twisting plots, transforming uncertainty
into moralised, anticipated endings –
mythology, poetry, fairy tale, legend,
soap opera, drama, reality TV –
showing us, teaching us how to be.

Then within us
was the word:
the bounce of heartbeat;
the red-flushed rush of blush
structured into already-formed sentences,
framing raw emotion
into the shape of words;
the repetitive rhythm of cliché;
the over-uttered of proverbial;
the ever-watchful eye of archetype;
the already ingrained
of arc, climax, anti-climax;
the expected restoration of resolution.

In the beginning
was the word.
We inherit the earth
already described, designated,
mediated, moulded,
meditated upon,
already forged into
the iron type-set of letter,
weighed, measured
into organised sounds
uttered by others
for centuries,
well-worn words
providing a thin skin
over everything,
attempting
to fashion the universe,
attempting to enunciate
infinity itself
within a limited, finite,
human arrangement
of sentence.

In the beginning
was the word,
and
the
word
was
God.

PAPATŪĀNUKU

I love that I've read
that Tangaroa was your first lover.
Despite the weight
of being primordial parents,
you lived other lives.

I imagine
the ways
you might have dissolved
in that salty saline water
where the edges of your bodies met.
The pull of those tides.

And then Rangi,
within that stifling, sensuous,
codependent embrace
– and beyond it –
the demands of children!
All that longing.

But I love best
that your bountiful body
is everything we land on,
stand on,
ground in.

You, woman,
are our go-to.
The earth under our feet.
The goddess that is all maunga,
all muscle, all soft slopes, fertile, flat surfaces.

You, Mother,
are home.

Papa – foundation, base: in twenty-six Austronesian languages.
Tū – to stand, arise, erect: in forty-five living languages.
Ā – Nuku – land, island, sand: in twenty Fijiac languages.

Papatūānuku – Goddess of all goodness.
Giving to us all, even the unworthy.
The absolute unconditional of you.

I could write about how we defile and despise you,
commercialise and divide you.

But that would be about us,
not about you.

Your serene resilience
rules supreme
in the face of what we chuck at you.

I could write about how violently the whakataukī changed
– at the end of guns of an army of empire –
from men dying and losing themselves completely
– over women and land –
Mā te wāhine, mā te whenua, ka ngaro te tangata.
To a legally binding adage whereby we all,
women and land
become the property of men.

Whereby the conceit of 'dominion over'
dominates.
But that would be about them,
not about us.

'Dominion over'
doesn't feature
in any of our epistemologies.

There are no single male creators
in any of our cosmogonies.
A man couldn't create on his own.

We made sense of our universe coming about
through co-creation, pro-creation, copulation,
where immensity and space were pulled to each other;
begat children.
The amino attraction
of male and female elements.

We are a family of relatives.
That includes the trees, the rocks, the sky and you,
Papatūānuku, are the mothership
of all the female elements.

And as much as 'the man' tries to bind you,
bend you to his will. You will resist.
That is one of your many legacies.

When we love on you
we love on ourselves.

When we pause,
in the busy noise of our days
and look to you,
we look to ourselves.

When we nurture,
tend and care for you,
we care for all of us.

In a world of lost goddesses,
my own Tongan darling
more lost than most,

Hikuleʻo, elder sister of Māui and Tangaloa,
desecrated, defiled, burned, beaten,
still found with the noose around your neck,
scattered sculptures overseas
the only proof of your presence
in museums and mausoleums.

Hikuleʻo, even in Wiki,
they've made you a man.
But the curves of your breasts
your beautiful belly,
your unmistakeable fertile places
endure beyond that lie.

When we honour you,
we honour ourselves,
we honour women
in all of our fullness,
wildness, wholeness,
power, tapu and mana.

Papatūānuku
– all of this
– all of us
– always.

When my flesh returns
to your soft soil, I too will become
a part of you, a sacred offering.
A sigh among many others,
that sweeps through the essence
of your many mauri.

All of this
all of us
always.

TE AWA: LOVE SONG FOR MANAWATŪ

The wind turbines
  wave their arms
    through
     the air.
    Sure strokes,
   they catch
  the current
still running electric
between Rangi
and Papa.

  Sky father,
    Earth mother.

   Rangi
    still weeps
   for his
  woman.

It is
rain
 upon
  rain.

  Each
   tear
    a tender
   drop
  on her
 muscled
body.

When the tips
of his tears
touch
the tops of
her tips,
her points,
her peaks,
her pulse,
it's all ebb and flow,
all over her body.

Ravine
like river
shaping
the nature
of her.

Her surfaces
smooth
under his
forever
flooding
feeling.

One of
these rivers
is
Manawatū
(named by
Haunui),
Manawatū,
where
the heart
stood still.

    So daunted
    at crossing
  a river
over-swelling
with emotion.

    Today,
      Manawatū,
      you carry
      not just
      the clean
      rain-soaked
      tears of Rangi,
but human waste,
fertilizer flows,
sewage, sediment.
  Our discharge goes
     into your beautiful body.

    Our excess,
     our unwanted,
     our never-ending flow.
    You carry it all in your
    beautiful, filthy body.

The burden we offer you
is too much
  for any one river
    to bear.

     Oh Manawatū,
     today my heart
     stands still
     for you.

We have all travelled through
   the bodies of many
      relatives to arrive here.

   All of us wearing
      those who have passed,
         fresh on our faces.

      We are the next waves of a tide
         that has been coming for a long time.

         Let us follow the ocean roads
           that lead us, via stars,
              to the expansion of each other.

           If we make mistakes on the shore,
              let us rectify this in the deep ocean.

              Let us steer through the storms.
                 for our leaders have always been determined,
                on the high seas.

                In times of darkness,
                  let us dare to shine
                  and have no fear
                    about burning too brightly.

                    Resist the dimming
                      and dumbing down
                        of low expectations.

                        It does not serve your families,
                          it does not serve our communities,
                          Let each of us find that place
                            where we have most to give.

MATAU
MANA
MOANA

Where we will be of most service.

   Resist those things that we fear
     and those people who fear us
        when we are at our most powerful.

      When the journey is too hard,
        let us tie our outriggers to each other
        and share breath.

          Let us heed the words of our ancestors,
            for the matau – the hooks – in your hands,
             which you use to cast your dreams,
              are hewed from the jawbones
               of your tupuna.

                  What do they want you to catch
                    in this lifetime?

                    What do you want your mokopuna
                      to catch in theirs?

                  You are the thread
                      between what has been before
                      and what will come,
                        as long as you have breath.

                      We have so much to remember.

                       We have much to learn.

                        We have so much to teach.

                         Let us serve.

MANA

How do I describe you in English

integrity / influence / respect / authority / none of those words / quite / reach

like the Greek word 'entheos' lies at the root of the word 'enthusiastic' / it means that / the gods are with you / creative / energetic / enthusiastic / charismatic / power / pulse

and yet mana / all of those words / fail to reveal you / although we all know / when you are gone

sometimes I imagine a personal bank / an accumulated pool of cool greenstone coins /
smooth to the touch
or layer / upon layer / of fine mats
or yard / upon yard of tapa
or gift / upon gift / on an altar of altruistic offerings / good deeds / awesome feats / IOUs /
a golden stash / not unlike cash / unbelievably good karmic credit
and yet this fails to describe / how you are more / than money / can buy

when mana walks in the room / it's instantly recognisable / intangible / expensive accessory / out of reach / it goes with all of your clothes / no room for cheap knock-offs / yet we all know / when we see someone / all mana / no money

mana / you are more than a precious stone on a neck

you are the space between / the performance / and the audience clapping
you are the ovation
we know it / when we see it
it ignites us / it alights us
so that the mana in me / sees the mana in you
remembering what it is to be exalted / connected
in conscious mind / with all that we are / all that we could be

and yet mana / you ebb and you flow / you come and you go
we live our lives / with / or without you

when you are with me / I am Māui who has harnessed the sun
gold burning through embered fingertips

I am all there / all energy
present / vital / awake
each cell singing an ode to being alive / woke

when you flow through my body / I know

I am caught in the current / of a river / larger than the length of my own lifetime
it bends where I have been before / same rapids / other waters
my veins / my blood
but I know / I am in the flow
of something greater than my own self
all of the earth / all of its gravity / physics / motion / movement
all of that / is with me
here / right now / time and space / making a place
for me / to be / all that is possible

and I am a few steps further / from the maunga / where I began as tears
one riverbank closer / to the ocean / where I will return
to saline / salt / water
all of that dream

return / to be burned by the sun / return
to be held by the clouds / return
to trickle down the stones of that mountain
return / all the way back to the river / and
flow

NGATU

Earth, sea, sky, wind –
cold pressed and beaten
into the paper-fleshed
nerve endings of ngatu.

This canvas carries
the changing of seasons;
the warp of hurricane;
the falling of leaves.
A whole sun cycle
forced into
materiality.
The bare-bark
of art.

Once we could translate
the text of the universe
memorise and mimic
the mosaic
of small movements
and make predictions:
trails of insects,
transit of birds,
swells of waves.
All of this
imprinted
on the muscle memory of masi
outlasting
human memory.

We have forgotten how to read the elements.
The instructions for fishing up land
are embossed
on siapo from Manuʻa.
The encoded maps
to gardens that grew us
are held in hiapo from Niue.
These song sheets
hold the lyric of lives
we've left behind.

You and I follow the fading
fingers of
the koka tree.
Tracing the distant dyes
that once wrote,
and interred,
the remains
and shapes
of our
original
names.

THE GOOD WIFE'S PRAYER

LONELY

I am lonely.

This truth seeks out the hollow,
finds its mark,
rests inside me.

It fills the curve of my ache
more than the question of
who loves me.

I am lonely

and do not have
a circle of women
to sit around me,
share
and meditate
their conscious will
into the world.

How I crave minds
like mine,
the tapa of connected talk
beating singular thoughts
and shame
into the symmetry
of company.

This talanoa
is both the rain
and the roof
we would gather under,
making us feel
both wild
and safe.

How I miss all of this
and all of you,
who I do not know
but need.

READJUSTING GREAT EXPECTATIONS

on good days
i expect nothing.
the secondhand scent
of remembered skin,
the warmth of the one
touching me.

on quiet days
the mixed tapes come out.
songs, long gone –
i still know all the words.

on empty days
I cut myself by picking up
the flutter of your eyelashes –
a library of dark curled arrows.

on bad days,
impossible feathers
try to take flight inside me,
hit the soft red walls of my body.
broken winged, we nest.

A WOMAN SCORNED

1.
I can feel
your face
turning away
turning a new leaf
reaching towards
a bright sun.

I imagine her
turning your
starch into
sugar.

Light energy
into chemical energy
into sweet glucose bonds,

the magic
of photosynthesis.

I am a fool
if I do not see
this is what life
is made of.

This is the air
that we breathe.

2.

Your limbs
are not indifferent
to my body
but I see the sway
away
from shade,

irretrievably
kinked
into your profile.

Each bend
a branching out,

in search of fairer
weather.

3.

I imagine
you felled.

Some sweet brown girl
will do it,
with kauri gum eyes,
toki in her brilliant
white teeth.

I imagine
you sawed
in half.

Someone
counting the rings,
each ring
thinking
she was the beginning
and end to her own
story,

not knowing
circumference
perimeter
bounds
limits
were shaped
by the ones
who went before.

Each of us
Babushka dolls
swallowed
by the other.

THE UNFAITHFUL HEART OF HER QUIET

Birds could have lifted the bones
from my wrists,
dry crusts
of daily bread.

This
crippled tree
cannot hold the weight of
fruit
fleshed with knowing.

How glossy
the carcass, the pelt, the fur
that is left of our bodies
on the floor.

How sad we are,
as dead as we are alive.
Carnivores, murderers,
husband and wife.

Mother and father.

BRUISE

Whatever happens,
you will leave a bruise
on me.

Red-bitten,
deep-sucking purple,
translucent blue,
faint black track marks,
vivid yellow halo.

Whether you touch me
or not,

the blunt
force
trauma
of want.

Every

time

I touch myself

it will

hurt.

TERMS OF A TREATY

The only
thing
society said
was

try

    harder.

We were expected
to be a faithful
rendition,

to be an excellent
iteration,

role models in
the performance
of a lifetime.

No
ambiguity in
the text that lay
at our feet,
dictating
a path
paved by
covenant,
written
into law
by forefathers
of Empire,
dictating
roles, rules,
predictability,
patriarchy.

What you are
allowed to rely on.

What you get.

This for that.

Terms of
reference.

Terms
of treaty.

Terms
of trade.

**Black
and white
penalties
of exit.**

Each page
turning
days into weeks,
an endless
serial.

A book
already
bound
and
written
to its end.

We were expected
to follow the
familial
arc all the way
to the end.

Typecast in
someone else's story.

An unsteady
pen
writing poems
of longing

in the margins
of my own life,

determined to
live my life
off the page.

ENTER HOT MAN AT AN INTERNATIONAL CONFERENCE
(FOR B)

When I met you
all my comfort was undone.

I was nothing but courage
and curves in a gifted dress
radiating self-discovery
emanating the heat of
following your bliss.

Even the Adelaide bricks were blushing
my skin solar, eyes dancing lights,
freedom flowing
faster than the wine
effervescently
full of shit.

You called it.

We looked and
saw each other

both contained
and overflowing,

recognised ourselves
as half-full
and half-empty.

Thirsty.
Lonely.
We drank.

ITINERARY OF INFIDELITY

Desire is crushed watermelon, fruit vodka, soda, lime and berry juice in a fiery red glass.

Escape is Peter Tosh dubbing on someone else's stereo, a deck opening out on a hot summer's day, the warm lush of it.

Anticipation is fat pigeons whirring in the bush, feathers flummoxing in chest, the arch of wings across shoulders.

Melting is his breath, feathery warm on my neck, a tongue curling; the space between two bodies thickens and chokes.

Passion is the licking of a breast in the kitchen of pure daylight, urging fingers slipped into rush of a body, the lure of taut tunnels, the slick luscious of delicious wet, the ocean open and flowing.

Intimacy is small histories bitten like ripe fruit straight from the tree, shared on tongues. Secrets unpeeled and sucked for sweet, fresh tang.

Adultery is the glowing flesh of apricots blushing hot in the sun, dribbling sticky in a pale blue glass bowl.

Tenderness is damp clay kisses to cool brows, the soft stroking of cheeks, the shining of eyes, the immaculate wonder of the other.

Destiny is black, muddy coffee, a river in flood, carrying black seeds, grimy, coarse in my throat.

Honesty is the silent push-me-pull-you of tandem breathing. It holds us, more purely than our words, less fraught than our skin.

In our quiet, the unspoken betrays us as truth.

SUMMER, BED, AWAKE, ALONE,

counting blessings can't send me to sleep, shoo flies from small bodies snoring, sounds of insect wings whirring, the soft sleep of charmed creatures

mind grinds through the movements, touches sharp agonies, same grazed knuckles, old aches, teeth worn from worry, a bed of smooth river stones

time tick-tocks with manic eyes, that wicked wick, incandescent, burning brightly at both

i want to reach out across the eight-hour drive, i want to snake past his sleeping wife, i want to slap him, i want to smother him, i want to shake him brilliantly, brilliantly awake

i want the kiss of death, i want to drop on his sword, i want to stop my heart, i want to shed my skin

love, love with its dark petals, blooming insomnia on a summer's night, pressing, pressing behind my eyes, dangerous dandelions with dreamy astronaut heads, a halo of possibilities, i want to break into a thousand parachutes, i want to be carried away by the wind

with night breath,

i wish,

i wish,

i wish,

i blow

LET ME TELL YOU WHAT I REMEMBER

Te reo spinning like a record across
the dance floor
Bob Marley T-shirts for Africa
reggae band from Ōtaki
kapa haka back-beat
it will be the sound of summer
for the rest of my life.

it was blacker than night
the rain attacked the house
as if to seal
the exchange
with spit

i remember
it hurt
the pushing
like a fist

an enclosed room
a painted black box
in a darker night

a white bird wings in
spinning around ceiling
in a frenzy / in a flutter

'my kaitiaki' he whispers
'checking you out'

i remember
it burned
afterwards

next morning
walking down his driveway
there was a little brown bird
by the letterbox

dead

WHIRO
(FOR S)

You have always been
my dark star,
upsetting
the evening sky
with your black-void-vacuum
brilliance,

the anti-star –
te korekore in the palm
    of your eye
emanating intensity,
your absence of light.

    Tender darkness
        truest
            reflection.

Oh, I was glorious and ordinary
in the daylight,
but you bade your time
in the shadows.

Prince of
Te Punga's
children,
reptilian
running cold
in your veins.

You came to me
in my dark unloved,

with a daughter of the moon
in your arms,
owls in your hair,
dark crescents
in your eyes.

A dark ocean inside of me
moved towards
that place
where you have always held me,

beyond time and space,
where you left a cavity
an abyss
an ache.

All my stars began combusting
in my night sky,

the ones we cannot see
with naked eye,

and I saw a vortex
still spinning
inside of you,
whirling
relentlessly,

its circumference
the size
of my
own
missing
shape.

I looked
    and loved

it was inevitable.

Could we circle back
to beyond our beginning

so two halves
could finally arrive
at a meeting place

where all Te Punga's children
will be gathered?

The lost, the lonely, the outcast

all of us
wondering
how we could
have ever subscribed
to a divide
that separated us
from them?

Yes
all will be gathered,
old spells will be broken,
myths will breathe beyond the page,
legends will walk among the living,
and old tapu binaries will collapse
beyond noa, into a new era.

You
and I
will
no longer be
you and I
in the
love.

Oracles
living to
see the
day.

LOVE ISN'T

Love is
fried rice
overflowing
with extras,
both prawns
&
bacon.

Not-love
is avoiding our four-legged table;
taking leftovers home
to sit cold in another woman's
fridge.

THE GOOD WIFE'S PRAYER

Let me be faithful,
first,
to myself.

Not betray
the essence
of who I am
for anybody.

Not husband,
son, father,
not mother
or daughter.

Let me believe
that being faithful,
first,
to myself,
is the ultimate
gift I can give.

Let me have the courage
to not just live a safe life
or a good life,
but a whole life.

Feel the full range
of feelings.

Let the energy
within my body
love what it loves,

attract what it attracts,

repel what it repels.

Let me be free
to be
me

in this moment,
here,

right now,

awake
and fully
present.

Let me
feel the
wairua
flow
through me
and greet life
in all
of its
unfolding
incarnations.

HAWAI'I

FOUND

WHAT THE STUDENTS SAID: OʻAHU 313

I asked the students of West Oʻahu
to tell me about their island
what they see, hear, taste, smell, feel?

Loud, busy, noisy they said.
The palm trees are fake.

Construction is in the air, everywhere.
Potholes at the end of every rainbow

They told me how military is spamming the land
with their sweaty, stinky, spy stuff.

They spoke of sitting in the car for two hours to get to town.

The time-consuming of laid-back and lazy.

They told me of imported ginger leis
woven by nimble Filipino fingers,
trapping tourists.
Airports chanting artificial welcomes.
There is no aloha to be found
in the seven shallow pools
of the Hilton Hawaiian Village.

They spoke of how sweetness
is found in their food:
poke, lilikoi, shave ice,
King's Hawaiian sweet bread.

Not one of them mentioned
a beach.

TŪTŪ PELE INTERVENES
(FOR MANULANI MEYER)

Daring, dazzling, dangerous:
the OG feminist, womanist,
whatever you want to call her.
Goddess will do.

Like all good goddesses,
she does exactly
as she pleases –
all subduction,
sweet talker.
'This is how you
get your groove back tita.'

Her fingers on the pulse of
tectonic pressure,
she feels the strike-slip
faulting.

She's pulling on
the alternate polarity of it.
Everything brittle
threatens to
fracture.

Pele, burning beloved.
Earth-eating woman
breaking through the bedrock.

'Reality bites tita.
Wake up. You've only got
one chance at life.'

She knows beneath
the earth's lithosphere
is softer, weaker cartilage –
the bone structure
of another face.

I dream her.

The frail places I stand
leaner, edgier,
every day.

I'm reduced to walking
on cooling piles
of molten magma.

Whole continents
don't work for me
any more.

With her hot lava hands
she
sends flow
into all of my empty.

Golden liquid
shifting,
shimmering
under hesitant heels.

Embers everywhere,
we wait
for something solid.

So I can step away
from safe.

OUR GENERATION: 'ĀINA ALOHA

(A COLLABORATIVE PAINTING BY MULTIPLE ARTISTS OF HAWAI'I COORDINATED BY MELE MEYER)

I peer into the painting –
see the past –
see the future –
but we are not there,
our generation.
We are kneeling
at a heiau of hope,
oli of old newspapers
on our tongues.

We carry our ancestors
in newsprint prayers:
overthrown, occupied,
annexed, imprisoned.

We offer up
everything
that we have of them,
hoping it will reach those
who have not yet arrived.

Moʻopuna.

We give it all up to the ʻiwa birds
rising translucent, transcending

i luna, i lalo,
above, below,

their boned wingspans
may
reach the promise
of what we hope for –

flight
in every direction.

Lele ka ʻiwa,
mālie kai koʻo.

When the ʻiwa bird flies out to sea
the rough will become calm.

Moʻopuna –
extensions of ourselves,
all that we dream,
the gifts of the future.

We can no longer gift them
certainty.

No, we are not there.
But we are no longer stuck
in the painful immediacy
of right here, right now,
without our history –
even though our heritage
of struggle, petitions of protest,
were hidden and housed
in microfilm,
in archives
on the mainland.

Sovereignty stolen,
tongues taken,
house-less in own home –
we are stripped even
of our acts of struggle.

As if we
chose
This.

History is always unwritten
by the victors.

But we will no longer
be mirrored back to ourselves
by poison pens –
bruised, broken,
raw, red,
although fresh blows
from an age
of empire
still land,
slap and bite.

A bloodless coup,
still bleeding.

We the wounded
can find ourselves
hurting everything
we love.

But, no, we are not there.
The eyes of our generation
are attuned
to the fractals
that break through
this illusion
to the other side.

For there are fault lines
in their pictures of us –
algorithms that do not add up,
a false mathematics, faked logic,
cruel calculations taught to us
as probable reality.

We do not see
the shining faces of our families
in their dusky images of us.
We will not be doomed
as devil-worshippers
by their brush.
Drifting, starving savages
lost at sea, in their
stretched canvases.
Barbaric cannibals in their
dark projections.

This is some strange
white-wash. We dream
through holographic holes
to the other side
to find our direction,
Hokuleʻa sails with us.
We have always
known the way.

He pūkoʻa kani ʻāina.

We are not there,
because we are holding
our own re-vision.

Paintbrushes in our hands,
drafting our dreams,
remembering the chants,
writing the poems,
relearning the language
composing the chants,
cooking the dinners,
carrying the children,
paying the bills,
fighting the fight,
with our tax-paying,
car-driving hands.

A collective of artists
narrating a story
we can bear to live in.
Creating an image
of ourselves,
we can love
to look at:

where we see
our own selves,

incarnations
of ancestors,

where we see
our own selves

moʻopuna
to come.

We, who write,
paint, sculpt, dance,
against all odds,

we make art
unconditionally

in these conditions.

We know that
all of us must heal,
or none.

INTERGENERATIONAL HEALING: LESSONS FROM HAWAI'I

At Maʻo farms
in Waianae,
even though
the river itself
has been stolen by the military,
the earth still gives bounty.
No pesticides
on her skin.
There, they return
to the soil,
begin again,
knowing
that we cannot rely
on the mono-vision
of mono-crop.
They let the earth
enjoy the diversity that is
her natural inclination.
Let her rest when she is tired.
Weed her gently
with well-worn hands.
Eat the fruits of the lands.

Harvesting
food sovereignty
along with the beans.
Sweating obesity
out.

The young here
are treated
for depression
with
Mycobacterium vaccae.
The serotonin release
found from

getting your hands dirty,
touching the earth
itself.

Actual jobs
and scholarships.
Hope
in a system
where jobs don't grow
on trees
and education is
not the mono-bullet
it promises to be.

Ancestors guide
through seasonal cycles.
We have all moved
through these rhythms
before, finding a
reliable beat.

This is food on the table.
Big dreams, small business.
Collective self-sufficiency.
Organic delivery.

Waianae:
saltwater swims
at end of a long day.
The blue healing
of all kinds of sore.

Almost everything natural
wants to heal you.
It is a remembering.

ANCHORING THE CRY FROM WITHIN

We are visiting
Kūkaniloko
Me, my mother, Mehana,
My boys asleep in the car.

We walk down the red earth road
I am barefoot
soaking up everything I can.
We approach the two
upstanding ancestors
in the form of rocks
swathed in light.

We stop talking.

We feel that thickness appear
in the air
particles
getting glutinous
something else is there
remembering,
breathing, being,
belonging, in a way
that you might interrupt
whatever it is, whoever they are,
that which cannot easily
be known.

Kapu.
You can feel it.

Mehana stands
at the feet of the two
her face towards the light.
We wait for the tourists
to walk past.

She begins,
teacher of chants,
chanting,
enchanting
the ancestors
awakening them
intentionally
to our presence.

We dare to be here.
We acknowledge you.
Mehana turns her

genealogy into
the shape of words
spoken,
name
after name,
so they know
who and how
and why.

I am grateful to be safe
under her mantle.

We approach
what Martha has already
dreamed out loud for me
stones arranged
already in my imagination
a poem already birthed
out of wonder.

Here we are
Mehana ushers the bottoms
of Japanese girls
off the rocks.

'*Sorry*'

Later we gather the
fruit, the leis, the money,
the offerings,
we strip the boulders clean.

'It's not our way,'
Mehana explains.

'They are just showing their love'
wanting to be part
of the mystery
that is us,
and not us.

Poem in hand,
I wonder if my words
are worthy.

We sit under a tree,
watch tourists
come and go.

Mehana has a knack
of repelling them.
They just knew.

We spend a long time
looking at the deep dip
in the mountain range,
where the sun sets,
in 'v-necked' glory
golden citrine
at the throat
of that mauka

Stunning.

Mehana speaks
about how the military
are only ones
allowed over
triangular dip

the one way
through
the mountains.

As if on cue
helicopters buzz
like black mosquitoes
overhead.

She tells me
Māui was born in Waianae.
I believe her.

Where else
would he be from?

A woman walks up
with her boys,
'Mehana.
It is me, Emma.'

They begin to
Ōlelo Havaii.
It is beautiful.

I stand
catch fragments
of its fluent echo.

Nod my head
at the pieces
I can piece
together.

I read them the poem.

It does not feel bad.

It is a remembering.

It is a ritual.
It is an offering
that does not need
to be cleaned
off the rocks.

They continue to
Ōlelo Hawaiʻi.

This then,
perhaps
is the
revolution.

To keep on
being ourselves
in a world
that is doing
everything it can
to change us.

KŪKANILOKO

Here, where the sky
spills its starry secrets,
caught and clenched
in the bouldered hands
of knuckled rock.

Here, where
the softly spoken
celestial signs of the
multiverse,
are hushed
and held
in a quiet
assembly
of stones.

Here, where
an earth compass
centres the galaxy
in the red navel
of Oʻahu.

Here, where Māui
could have snared the sun
umbilical cords stretching
skylines connected
to calendar stars
harnessing time and space
to interpret the
future of a
generation.

Here where
a waʻa of stones
sails the blood red soil
north-west
toward the
setting sun.

Here where
a compass rock
is used to
navigate the night
sail the black
shining road of Kāne
stepping stones
into dark waves
of the undulating pō.
anchored
by eight
sun stations.

Here, where
the fire ring of aliʻi
burns upright
as the navel cords
of destiny
are cut.

Here, where
the dagger
shadows fall
on reckoning stones,
and hot blazes of fire,
are born to rule,
with their
burning backs
of kapu,
ablaze
anticipated,
celestially selected,
the comets of flesh.

The big drums are beaten
when the glowing ones
return.

All of us
still waiting
for the shining ones
to reappear.

DEMIGODS IN ARCHETYPE CITY

SHARK

NEVER OFFER YOUR HEART TO A POET.

NEVER OFFER YOUR HEART TO A POET.
Well-dressed words
strolling down her
red-carpet tongue,
a conch shell dress
in Hawaiiki-beach white.
Coral combs in her hair,
skin soft as sand,
all leading to a white balcony
of shark teeth
shining in her mouth.

NEVER OFFER YOUR HEART TO A POET.
She can go fishing for feelings
with a translucent string of letters
and catch something inside you,
substantial enough
to feed a family of four.
Abalone flashing in dark eyes,
courting the fire-walking,
shark-hunting,
dangerous things men do.

NEVER OFFER YOUR HEART TO A POET.
Her luggage full of glittering, glistening
metaphors, a make-up bag full of
scented oils, soft-smelling creams,
sharp literary devices,
machete, war club, machine gun,
set on repeat.

Hina has handmaidens
and seahorses,
hand-mirrors of
rear-view autobiographical
verse.

If you hear the moon mentioned,
step back.

You don't want to learn
the hard way
that writing fiction means
she never has to admit
she's lying.

HINA: ADVICE COLUMN ACROSS THE AGES

Dear Lonely-Heart,

Haters gonna hate,
players gonna play.

What's a good looking
girl to do?

This much I know.

Never trust a
two-faced archetype.

The size of his whale
is secondary.

Even if he makes
your toes curl,
your hips swirl,
your eyes fluorescent,
dark hair iridescent,
don't trust the slow glow
of your own excited skin.

Don't let him in.

Don't let the fine mats
woven with silken thread
turn your head.

Tell him to stick his red feathers
where the sun don't shine.

Don't listen to the lines
that fall from his mouth,
baited hooks dangling.
Don't let that meat anywhere
near your mouth, girlfriend,
or your fate will be bait
for his next angel.

Watch out for the wives
he never told you about.
Three's a crowd,
but four under one thatched roof
can be a covenant
for murder.

They don't know
who they're messing with.

I'm not a shark
personification
for nothing.

And my own sexual subterfuge?
That irresistible sharp pointed fin?
Indicating sin?

It all comes full circle,
some slapper a couple of islands away
and girlfriend, I told you,
players gonna play,
but my heart broke that day,
although I'm no prototype angel,
that's not my calling,
but lonely heart,
I was falling,
reeling, keeling,
woman overboard,
the sinking wounded,
the winded woman,
I was the gasping fish
out of water,
salt up her nose,
sweat in her clothes,
that woman's smell
on everything.

Therefore dear Lonely Heart,
Don't do as I do, but do as I say.
Pay attention, instead,

to what my Daddy once said,
'the only one you can truly trust
is your tuna.'

The eel who'd crawl on his belly
under your elegant dancing toe.

Find yourself a man
who would cut off his own head.

Plant it to please you,
to clothe and to feed you.

Coconut: fruit, nut and seed,
all that you need
for ever-after.

Lonely Heart,
drink to the memory of that
ultimate sacrifice.
In death, giving life,
a sweet saline sacrament,
a creamy offering,
flesh of his flesh
put it in on your tongue
and give thanks.

Put your lips to that cold mouth
that will tell you no lies,
look into those dark, wooden eyes,
kiss the brow of that nutted forehead.
It's so much easier,
dear lonely heart,
to love the dead.

THE TALE OF HINA AND SINILAU

There's always another side to the story;
always another face to the name.
Tigilau, Tinirau, Sinilau,
Janus, Gemini.
No matter what language you speak,
you're likely to be double-crossed.

Dark, lovely cowrie-shell eyes,
who'd expect the lies,
unless you flipped that fragile shell over
to the serrated crack
of the backside,
where the sea slugs reside,
that weak pink flesh on the inside.
Everyone's got a living surprise,
the part that they hide.

He's the heartbreak hero,
two Cupid arrows
stretching in opposite directions.
One follows the sun trail of his golden words,
dappled fontanel opening up to the light.

The other arrow points down
to the penultimate dark
of the other nadir,
to the piko between your legs.

He avoids the navel gazing in the middle,

doesn't like
what he might see,

avoids introspection,
considers himself an exception.

How long could it have lasted?

The insularity of mutual affection,
the perfect polarity
of opposites and attraction.

Having your way with her,
living to play with her,
big fish in small pond.
Existing only for each other
within four rock-lined walls –
pooled pleasure.

Manifestation into two-legged man
didn't quite go to plan.
All of a sudden,
he's gone fishing.
Narphal-nosed,
thick-skinned,
but still wounded
by the wild shark
he sea-bedded.

And before long,
he's dipped and finned
his way into other,
hooking the easiest option.

There's the family dinner for four
and what he eats at lunchtimes.

Perhaps his fate
to take that bad bait.

Tinirau, the hopelessly
two-legged.

Everything is raw.
It's a fish-fight, it's fuckery,
it's a frightening mess.

She learns the bitter taste
of that cockle.

Swallows it.

Everything was so much easier
when he was eel
in her oiled hands.

The other woman's mussel
still on his breath.

The sting-rayed barb of betrayal.

Silver scales slip
down her cheeks.

Inevitably, she cries
an ocean.

HINA AND HER POOL

She stares at her reflection.

Sees everything that is not there.

Her whole life mirrored back to her
in tiny, broken, undulating portions –
ripples of distortions.

The murmurs of this moving mirror –
seven thousand small years of bad luck.

The pool catches the face of a fresh flower,
reflects it back – blurry, bent, broken.

Even strong trunked trees
bend and sway in the small waves.

They wave their wobbly arms,
chin up, chin up –

*all is not what it seems
in this liquid looking glass.*

Each leaf urges and ushers her,
*get out, get out, get out,
look away,* they say
life is happening elsewhere.

But she is compelled to stay,
searching for answers
in the stagnant waters
of what was.

RUPE/LUPE

You will find yourself
calling out the name
of that brother
who annoyed you every day.

He will hear the cry of his sister,
transform his gangly body
into proud pigeon chest.
Beaked determination,
feathered shoulders,
avenging angel.

He will make his way
towards Motutapu
where the shit has hit the fan.

He will swoop down and sweep you up,
cradle you in his soft wingspan,
take you home, ocean roads.

Brother: his manifestation
from boy into bird into man.

Giving flight to
a two-winged covenant –
Feagaiga,
Faka'apa'apa.

Twinned fate.
Brother serving sister ...
her honour,
his honour,
evermore.

Rupe, Lupe is his name,
winging his way
into his calling.

Bending the bones
of his own perfect
becoming.

WHAT TREES WILL SAY

Be still,

lean towards the light,

reach towards everything.

Anything living
to please itself
is perfect.

Everything wild
survives
by accepting
every aspect
of themselves
and their surrounds –

adapting.

Being yourself
is the best beauty.

The flower of you			There is nowhere else to look.
is often best
unplucked.

Some mortal man
will come
try and carve
his initials into you.

You will outgrow him.

You belong only
to the wind and the sun,
the soil and the rain.

The seeds to your regrowth
come from your own branches.

ONE LAST

LIFETIME

DRY-DOCKED

There is a sweetness
in that last memory of you
all dressed up in black
in my kitchen.

You'd spent eight hours
crawling through the guts
of a two million dollar boat.

I hope you understand
that no matter how long I slept alone
I could not have crawled on my belly
to find out exactly
how the small parts
moving
and ticking
inside of you,
with all their quake
and silent motion,
ordered, and arranged
any thoughts of me.

I could not ask.

I could not make sense of,
how you made
sense of,
us.

In the looking glass
I prefer the
swan necked
version of self,
elegantly not

giving a smooth
white crap
about what you
did
or did not
feel.

Even this poem is a betrayal.

Although, truth be told
I'm as much
beak-in-the-muck
as the next bird,
wanting to get
down in the dirty
into the henpecked
truth of it.

But I will
sway away
every time.

Lean towards
the graceful
long-necked
ambivalence
of a single
white feather
rather than
lean in
and risk.

Even this poem is a betrayal.

All I know
is that in those rare days
where there is no future
and no past,
just the hand-cupped
moment
of seawater
held in both palms,
that I blew wishes
from above
like an out-of-body
all-seeing angel,
a poorly timed gust of love
upon a small
but seaworthy boat
that missed the priest's blessings
but caught my own.

I blew gently
on non-existent sails
wishing we could have
gone somewhere
past the red rocks
to beyond blue
to somewhere far-flung and green
with white coral beaches
closer to where I come from
where it is both warm
and ancient.

There, where voyage
is not dictated by
the tight linear mathematics
of latitudes and longitudes
of age, distance, or destination.

Where there is no need for calculation
of where things might go
over the years,
no need for predictive map
careful compass or precise GPS.

There, where we could look to the stars,
tides, moon, birds and skies,
see the alignment
and trust.

Trust
that at the very least
we could defy
ordinary directions.

But we live here, where
our hands can only be held
underwater
for the sweetest salt-soaked dive.
In ways
I could not imagine
in the wide-eyed dry.

Whatever it was,
bittersweet
between us,
it did not easily fit
in the oiled machinery
of the expected
in the non-stop
watertight world
ruled by time.

A wishbone
between my ribs
that could
catapult
from it's bow-legged arcs
something soft
and undetermined
into the choke
of the thick unspoken
between us.

Late nights
on my couch

it silently shanghai'ed
the briefest
of shooting stars –
bright and near death –
glowing with impending
short-lived light,
into the dark-eyed
between us.

The quick combustion
of an alternative universe.
Both possible
and impossible.

That wishbone
stuck words
in my throat,
that never made it past
lips
absolutely
unkissed.

I can live with that,
as long as everything
remains
beautifully intact,
and completely
my own.

But this poem
is a betrayal of that.

For there is a part of me
that wants to go
all the way
out to sea.

It frail wishbone
split into the shape
of Y.
Two-tailed, two-trailed,
a forked park
in the tiny tangle before me.

Most miniature
of anchors,

it holds you,
so very quietly,
close.

When that wishbone
finds it wings:
it is two kāhu circling,
the dark-eyed deep,
so very near the peak
of Pukeahu.

Pukeahu,
it will always be
a standing reminder
of what was,
what wasn't,
what is remembered,
what is imagined,
and what is lost to us.

WEDDING RIVER SONG

(COMMISSIONED BY MY NANA FOR NEWLY-WEDS)

Beside you,
   I feel that the best of myself,
      free-flowing,
         might arrive,
            and my compassion
               might not run dry.

        Even when the rivers run low,
     in your presence
    is the promise of rain.

It is in the dew
   of little daily things,
      that we are refreshed.

     If we are lucky,
    in the everyday water
   of another,
  our thirst
is quenched.

  Even when the rivers run low,
    what more can you ask for
     than to find flow,
       with someone heading
         in the same direction.

       What more can you ask for
     than company,
      on this journey
        from mountain to sea,
     at every bend, a friend.
    No longer alone,
    when what is stone
   turns to flowing.

And we have to find our way through
the parched and cracked parts of ourselves
found in life's dry and killing seasons,
and we are pushed to find reasons
to keep on going.

Let this river then,
running between us,
be wide enough
and deep enough
to carry all that it needs to hold,
so that we know the grace of flow,
the blessings of buoyancy,
and the cool waters of each other
at the end of a long day.

Let me put you to my lips and drink.

Give us the patience
to find each other
in the still waters
of our silences.

Give us alignment
with the undercurrent of each other
so we can understand
the white breaking waters
on the surface.

Give us the skills to soothe
each other through
the soreness
of our lows.

And at our absolute heights
   when our banks runneth over
      with laughter and love and abundance,
         let us be life-giving to all we touch.

      Let us bring out the best not only in each other,
     but in all that we meet and greet.
    So all that is fertile will flourish,
   and all that is dry can be nourished,
   and we can plan and plant gardens
     that will feed not only each other,
       but those beyond our boundaries.

       Together, let us plant trees
         that grow beyond the length
        of our own lifetimes
           and shelter generations to come.

        Let us sow seeds
           at the start of this new beginning,
             on this journey from the peaks of the mountain
         to the vastness of the sea.

    Let us follow the course of the river,
In this life,
come flow with me.

IS THAT A SEX POEM?

Even a cynical, overpriced Auckland sky
reduced to real estate,
and bitter about it,
is alight with delight tonight.

Tāmaki Makaurau
silking itself up
on a Saturday night.
State Highway 16,
swallowing clouds of dark
with a soft and trembling
blue mouth.

Tonight there was thunder,
strange yellow fluorescent
damp moonlight,
rainbows skidding sideways on tarmac –
pearlised shellac.

I'm driving through the new Waterview tunnel
away from you, towards poetry.

And even as I'm leaving,
I'm moving towards you.

That's how it is now.

The sky is moody
and ready to roll me.
Even the tunnel
has got its multimillion dollar glow on,
going on and on,
longer than you expected.

Expensive.

I hard-left for hard-west,
not soft-west where I live,
so central.

It's a sudden, wide-eyed sunset,
swimming with sea light.
That motorway is ramming
through the throat of the ocean.
Wind down your windows,
smell the salt air,
feel the water edging you,
nudging up against your elbows.

When I catch myself later
in the Town Hall mirror out West,
unexpectedly reflected back to myself,
my hair looks like it's been
under sheets.
My cheeks all afterglow.
I can still taste the rain of you
silking itself up
in my trembling mouth.
Ocean throat
full of damp starlit magic.

I am remembering
the ready-to-roll
of white sheets.
Brilliant collision
in open-skied bed.

That's how it is right now.
Even as I'm leaving,
I'm moving towards you.
You are everywhere
on my horizon –
shadow in my side mirrors.
In the open-mouthed motorway,
through the tunnel
via the hard-turn,
in the wet
of Waterview.
In the wide-open spread
of the Waitakere ranges.
In the sticky sunset of the city sky.
You are everywhere.
Even as you leave me behind
in the Auckland massive.

GO-BETWEENS

We are perched on stools
in Kokako Café,
pecking on agria hash,
avocado and eggs.

Birds swarm in all of our stories:
pīwakawaka, kāhu, rūrū;
messengers, miracles, manu.
The up-to-the-atua
and back-again of them.

The birds are the
go-between.
We all
instinctively
know this.

In the migrating flight
of whakapapa
we can remember
how we have been them.
The birds, our ancestors,
broken wing sockets
in our arched shoulders,
the ache, the dull, two-legged
of here.

In Kokako Café,
we three speak of love,
using sports metaphors,
and of the times
we wanted to die,
and of tohu and new lovers,
the dead and ex-husbands,
and finding arms
in which we can nest.

I think about the time,
but do not tell it,
when you and I saw
the two kāhu in the sky,
'Do you see them?' you asked.

It was right at the beginning of us.
We were in the boring of the office.
I watched them at the huge window,
the way they were moving.

And you stood brilliantly
quiet next to me.
And for the first time I wondered
if maybe, you were meant for me.

It is only now I know,
those kāhu were doing
a courtship dance,
and who knew?
Not you nor I
at the time.

A bird of prey –
our good omen.

I saw them
swirling all around us –
signs, signs, everywhere –
smashing themselves against my windows,
breaking mirrors,
even flying fish.

When I finally speak out loud
to the others,
it is to voice my fears
about the unfeathered ones,
the creatures
that move in the trees at Ōwairaka,
the ones that come to swallow you at night.
It is dreamtime
that is the most dangerous.
The dark dawn chorus
of the dead.

She turns to me gently and says,
so much kindness in her eyes:
My uncle always said,
Never mind those who have died.
It will be the living ones
who kill you.

BLOODSHED

Since we've become lovers,
I have lost so much blood.

A steady stream.
A trickle-down effect.
A drip feed.
My lifeblood
on tap.

An awa toto.
I am this river.
This river is me.

Something
 is bleeding
  like fresh kill
   inside of me.

Something
 is bleeding
  like new birth
   inside of me.

Every time
we are apart
I begin to bleed.

We are
always
apart.

This period
 has gone on
  too long.

I see the doctor.
She says
this could go on for months.

I reach for the iron tablets.
I drink the bitter potion
made by the witch
at organic wholefoods.
She writes my name on the bottle.
She takes my date of birth.

I sip.
I swallow.
I bleed.

This happened to me
once before.
A long time ago.
First love.
Red blood.
White sheet.
A whole summer
without him.

I bled until
he broke
me.

That summer
I turned seventeen
I could turn a full bathtub
red as roses.

They say the first cut
is the deepest
But here I am,
haemorrhaging again.
Amuia le masina, e alu ma sau.

Moon, I watch you out of the corner
of my attention span.
We wax and wane
deplete and drain,
but still we rise.

With trembling fingers
I insert a soft cup inside me
it swells like a ripe tulip.
Every few hours
I empty a full purse,
dark falling petals
a red mulled offering
free flowing.

My blood
a fresh
live sacrifice
to the goddesses
of high expectations,
to the narrow gods of
harsh judgements,
to the matakite who,
all three, foresee disaster.
Not tika. Not pono.
Consequences
for the children.

Everywhere expresses their disdain.
Even ordinary oracles of
Definitely. Don't.
Do. That.

Small red warnings
appear
like bloodstains
in my pants.

Yes, I know, I say,
I may be too old for this boy.

Yes, I know, I say,
I have a brand-new baby to another.

Yes, I know, I say,
a household will break in half.

Yes, I know, I say,
I have fine young sons
ripe for the reaping.

But please

I just can't
not

any more.

Can you
let us

want
what
we want,

need
what
we need,

love
what
we love?

Just until
we can
stop.

It's already done.

My own blood
on my hands.

CARVED ON A POU

[73. HOUSE POST, SOLOMON ISLANDS, OCEANIA EXHIBITION, ROYAL ACADEMY]

Let them say,
  where we once loved,
    fresh water
      can still be found
        there.

      Let them think of us,
        when the king tides come,
          and the earth and sun
            and the sun and moon
              come closest to touching.

              I remember when we first met,
                all those generations ago.
                Crab and lizard –
                  our first incarnation
                    of longing,
                      breaking tapu
                        from the beginning.

                So many
                  lifetimes.

You and I,
  crossing bloodlines,
    gender, age, race,
     fluidity, flowing
       across time and space.
         Transcending every
           breath-taking rule.

             Transcending
               every disruptive
                 death.

                   The joy of finally
                     finding your face –
                       the relief of return.
                         Finding ourselves
                           fully alive
                             again,
                               in each other.

                                 Oh beloved,
                                   all I ever wanted
                                     was a dark-haired daughter
                                       to breathe
                                         us on.

                                           All I ever wanted
                                             was one last
                                               lifetime together,
                                                 so that by the end of it
                                                   we could say,
                                                     we were almost
                                                       ourselves
                                                         again.

YOU'VE WRITTEN A LOT OF POEMS, HE SAID

You've written a lot of poems
he said.

Yes.

It's how I turn mess
into tidy.

How I organise chaos
into clean.

It's how I turn
self-harm
into
black blade
on white page.

The written stutter
of hesitant hurts.

The incoherent hiccuping
into glottal stops of admissions.

The staccato of sobs
sounding themselves out.

Each taking their breath
and holding it.

Staking out their turf
one surveyor's peg
at a time
into the land
of the living.

Into the land
of out loud.

It's how I turn shame
into something
that can bear
to be barely
seen

transforming
the amorphous of
unbelievably needy,
into shapes
I can claim
as my own.

Half dignified
movements
– so many of them
towards you.

My hopeless
and hopeful
lean in,

twinned,
embarrassed
refusing to look you
in the eye.

The sly
sinking
of shy
feeling

into shadow words
in narrow corridors
of shady alleyways
that slink and slant
and lie in wait
with bated breath
to see if they'll ever
see light
of day.

It's how I turn fear
into the careful tread
of light footstep
of word,
followed by light footstep
of word,
a trail that moves so fast
and leads quickly back
to my trembling
centre.

It's how I transform all the
mess, chaos, self-harm,
shame, fear into poetry.
all the too hard
into softly spoken.

All the ugly
into beautiful.

Oh beloved,
It's my only trick.

ODYSSEY IN BLACK SAND

1)

Windswept, alone,
transformed and free.
Sounds like a black beach
I have only walked upon
for a few afternoons,
never staying to see it through
beyond dusk
into uncertain.

The sea here
is too dangerous
to swim in.
Curdled green-blue
head-bashing into white,
wrestling in every direction,
deeply muscled waves
rip tides, thick spit, swirling hips,
saltwater saturated,
spindrift sweat.
It's a fight out there. Perilous.
Seagulls keep their distance
from the swirling surface.

Taniwha
petrified
look out
to ocean.
Perpetually
keeping watch
for what might come
from the far horizon.
Rear hind legs rocked.
Bracing themselves
in crouch.

This all imprints indefinitely
into my definition of wild.

2)

My best friend
walks this world
on the daily.

Dark, dazzling, free
windswept curly kelp:
there's always a party
to be had
in her black-sequinned handbag.

Older sister,
she replays a soundtrack
to a new movie
I could see myself
starring in.

Taking a drag on her cigarette,
she gifts me a dress
to wear –
discarded gown,
fairy godmother.

We angel-walk
the beach.
Sun hits the black,
and we are on a spinning planet
in a galaxy of mystery:
sparkling mini metropolis
of broken miracles
at my feet. The remix
could be a shifting dark
kaleidoscope of possibilities

Like a wise woman,
she spies my escape
from a life I am no longer willing
to live in.

She speaks it out loud
like a spell.

I'm intoxicated
with the feeling of freedom.

But I can't believe
in my
own magic.

I think: I will walk away,
again, towards nothing I want.

But what would I become
if I stayed long enough
to know the terrain
in its wholeness?

Became familiar with the routines
of tide, come to know
the gestures of birds,
followed the stark light
techniques of the sun
until I discovered markers
of a different time?
It is a seductive
hot black glitter
trail
back
to myself.

Can I tell that girl
not to walk away?

Place heavy orbs of sand
in her hands
and say
stay.

Sinkers.
So she weights
long enough
to confront
my own
dark swirling
company?

Each whispering
dark grain of sand
is mouthing myself
back to me:

Girl,
stop. sit. still. listen.
let all the noise die down
so we can talk.

3)

My black glittery muse,
two steps ahead of me,
smoky halo,
speaks
truth into my life.

I play that soundtrack.
I wear the dress.
I fall in love.
She approves.

I toast to my freedom,
take her hand,
my beautiful lover
in the other.

I'm in the movie.

But the voice I hear
– each dark grain of sand –
sounds like hers.

Sequinned. Cocktailed.
Drugged. Clever.
Playing goddess.

She speaks
truth into my life,
wielding it
like westerly wind.

She speaks: a whip,
a thrashing, a beating.
Smoke and dark mirrors.
A gaslit dance. Sand-storm.
I am blinded.

She speaks
truth into my life
until it starts to sound
like lies.

Secrets are
stealth bombs of choice –
weapons out of the mouth
of my babe.

Not hers to share.
Poison. Betrayal.

For-my-own-good.
For-his.

He is deathly silent.

I draw a circle around myself
in the black sand.

Boundaried.

I scream.
I separate.

4)

I walk wounded
into the water.
It's fight.

Deep, in dark muscled tide
thrashing kelp,
trying to keep
afloat. Perilous.

I have already lost
what I loved most in the world.

He holds on to her
with both hands.
She is all life raft.
Rescue.

They stand twinned
nodding heads
on dark shore.

I am buried
in a ritual,
in her back yard.

Know, you were loved.
I cannot believe.

But these are
ancient
and infant
eruptions – underfoot:
a forensic flow of fractures,
old bones, injury, memory
dismembered here and
disassociated,
discarded, squandered
trauma-bonded,
in impossibly
blue-black-hearted
sinking sand.

It will take more than one lifetime
to understand.

I turn my back.

Be-witched.

5)

An ocean
of alone.

Ever after
feels like
underwater.

Months pass,
treading
loneliness.

Rip tides carry me
so far out to sea –
the tide
brings me back
eventually,
always
alone.

One
day
runs into
the wave
of another.

Until,
from the deep,
I hear a siren singing.
Ka ū, ka ū, ki uta.

A song meant for me,
but I could not hear it.

Listening only to her.
Ascribing enchanted
to him.
Ka ū, ka ū, ki uta.

In my deep silence,
she sings me
slowly back to myself –

mouth-to-mouth
hands pressing hard
and rhythmic on my chest.

Hiʻiaka, Pele, Lohiʻau
ancient trinity,
watch over.

I choke, we float.

We climb on the back of a shark: Hina.
Grandmother turtle at side.
Stingray as guide.
We enchant our way
through the water.
Ka ū, ka ū, ki uta.

Exhausted,
with shaky knowing,
we emerge
on the other side.

Heavy orbs of sand
in empty hands.

Finally,
I say,
I understand.

I stop. I still. I listen. I wait.

When I hear her voice –
I recognise it
as my own.

Re-membered.
Old bones gather. Intended,
Re-guarded. Mended.

When my voice speaks,
it is the breaking of
splitting stone.

It roars.

Roars like a taniwha.
that has waited
a long time
to come
home.

There is not a kāhu to be seen
in this tauhou sky.

Kārearea
appears
right on time.

We take my words back.
We take my power back.
We take my heart back.
We take myself.

Ka ū, ka ū, ki uta.
And they sing:

We shall come
ashore in you.

You shall eat the heart
of this strange land.

You shall eat the heart
of the world of light.

Know
that those people
are not your medicine.

HOW TO BREAK A CURSE
(FOR N)

Go outside
Stick your feet in the mud.
Papatūānuku will feel your aching,
burning, angry organs.
Let her soft clays cool you.
Ground.

Feel what is solid under your feet.
Feel what is slippery.
Find your balance.
Thank it.
Ground.

Stand in the rain.
For hours if you need to.
It's a good start.
Wash yourself clean.
All that water from the sky above.
Cleanse.
Thank it.

Go to the river.
Go under if you can.
Let the rushing rapids take the muck away.
Let it carry what it needs to.
Cleanse.
Thank it.

Climb a maunga.
A volcano will do.
Look out, look out
over the width
and length of your life.
Get perspective.
Feel how much it could be.
Nothing small.
Dream it all
at your feet.
Thank it.

Nourish yourself
Sip on soups and fresh water,
eat softly steamed vegetables.
Remember those people
are not your medicine.
Don't swallow their words.
Do not let the spite
enter your body
in small, carefully
measured teaspoons.
Forage for fruit, suck on all
the sweetness you can find.
Gather your strength,
send goodness
all through your body.
Thank it.

Get out of your house. Find a forest.
A place where trees gather
together and just be.
Lean on a trunk.
Wrap yourself around it.

Let its branches feel your pain.
It knows how to bend
in the wind and the rain
without breaking.
Sun and seasons
baked onto its skin,
absorbing everything.
Let that tree feel
your frayed nerves,
cellular stress, carbon-heavy
deep breath.
Let it absorb it.
Let it pull it all up
through its living body,
and transform it
into air you can breathe.
Breathe.

Knowing it is life-giving.
Let it tell you of seasons,
how they come and go,
that this too will pass.
Let its deciduous nature
remind you too,
of what is evergreen
inside you.
Thank it.

As for the small darts
they send from afar,
intending to damage
and wound,
small negative intentions
of envy, poison,
and undisciplined hate ...

Lean on the bark of that tree,
let it wrap its arms around you,
let its elbows shield you
with its effortless togetherness.
Let it feel all of your pain.
Be the soft, sobbing child
curling in its arms. It's okay.
Nobody likes this.
Let the light shine through its leaves,
hear cicadas and their rhythm ease,
feel the soft breeze, ask for all that grows
and thrives to protect you.
Thank it.

Walk fearlessly into the night.
Barefoot and brave.
Look into the wide eye of the moon.
Invite her to shine; allow it.
Place stones around your home,
and snare her energy,
to keep light in –
unwanted out.
Let the darkness that gathers
with its ugly voices of doubt
and fear, finally murmur,
and hush. It has taught you
what it needs to.
Ask it to mindfully leave.
Thank it.

Go to the beach.
Stand on the shoreline.
Untangle and untie
that messy net
that somehow still
snares you there. Stuck.
Those small, carefully tied
knots of negativity.
Bless the hands
that pull the strings;
tie the tension
that binds you there.

Clear.
Cut it loose.
Remove the noose.
Unbind. Forgive.
Forgive yourself
for the small, little mistakes
and betrayals
that still catch you
at the ankles.
Let them go.
As you release them
from the fault, so
you are unbound.
Free.
Thank them.

Watch the water.
Wade in.
Fully clothed if you need to.
Let the waves whack you
with all their pulsing energy
and power. Feel everything
crash and churn until
it starts to subside,
feel the rip tide ease.

The stinging salt
does different things
to the sweet water.
Let it cleanse you.
Thank it.

Come home.
Light a candle
for the lightness
that you require within.
Light a candle
for the brightness
that you need to be.
Light a candle
for all
that has loathed you.
You have grown so much.
Evolved. Stretched. Hurt. Healed.
It is free to leave now,
there is nothing more to learn.
Thank it.

Go to your bedroom.
Put kawakawa balm
in that big hair of yours
and shake it
into the only net you now carry,
the threads that whakapapa
you back to all
that will protect you.
Thank them.

Brush out the knots.
remember these connections
that take you all the way back
to the first strand.
Surround yourself with a circle;
heal each other with
truth, tears, laughter.
Those people
are not your medicine.
Thank them.

Say a prayer.
all we ask for
is to rise,
the way the sun does,
with very little effort,
ease, each day.

Ask for that blessing.
That's their medicine my friend.

That daily dose
of all they never
wanted you to be –
of all they hoped
you couldn't have –
of all they were
secretly envious of –
of all they wanted you
to be alone in.

And you
so grounded.
You so free.
You so radiant and radiating.
You, the full-mooned
version of yourself.

All light, light, light.

You. A maunga inside.
A circle of good around you.
Standing tall
at a new shoreline,
a new net in your hands.
You, scoping the open horizon,
seeing signs
you've never seen before.
Birds muttering directions
under beak breath, watchful eyes –
are you watching?

Yes, yes, for the first time,
you are.

You,
swaying tall and gentle
with the trees,
tending to the mystery
of your own mauri.

Your children so safe
in the strength of your
forgiving branches,
absorbing it all for them,
naturally.

Ready,

oh so ready,

to launch yourself

at life.

OTHER
SIDE

TELLING THE OF THE STORY

AFTER READING *ANCESTRY*

(FOR ALBERT WENDT)

Page by page,

I found my dreaming, padding feet
in the lush green grass of Mānoa, Hawai'i,
sand under surveillance at Long Bay,
at the table of Palagi breakfasts in Samoa,
circling an unfamiliar umu pit.

But all roads lead to Ponsonby
where restored villas ascend,
skylighted, into lagituaiva,
and the leaves still speak
the gentle green-tongued talk
of tended gardens.

You, Albert,
character among your characters
appear, a dreaming woman
at your side, flourishing.
The soil of stories in your hands.

You kneel together,
planting the strangers of our sleeping lives.
Past and present collide
in one single kernel,
unfolding beyond the boundaries
of dream. Taking their own shape,
orbiting out into a garden

of pūkeko, people, aloe vera, eels,
light, lettuce, mokopuna,
named fine mats,
feijoas, family gods, fungus
and freedom trees.

We are all permanent guests
of landscapes you've created.
The nuances of red
bloom. The caramel generation grow,
practised schizophrenics, surviving
the small humiliations of raw peripheries.

You've traversed it all,
charting outsider territory
with black star
after black star.
before us.
The relief of
another way of mapping.

Death will come
and still your garden will grow,
owls circling softly overhead.

Once you've imagined it possible
to gafa back to Atua,
the story can never be the same again.

SON, FOR THE RETURN HOME
(FOR MAKA TOA)

My son, for the return home,
where will that be?
The Tonga that I offer you
with a mouthful of burning poems,
like a second-hand story,
the never-never land of school holidays
fished out of the moana by Māui,
given to God.

Where you are more likely
to bump into Moses, Abraham or Judas
on any given Sunday
than Māui, Hikuleʻo or Tangaloa.

As storytellers, we are the makers
and breakers of the dreams of gods,
our demigods cartoon fodder
for the next Disney movie.
The Tongan Māui was split
into three-way male archetype:
old, middle-man, young
(Māui Motuʻa, Māui ʻAtalanga, Māui Kisikisi).
Poor Māui ʻAtalanga,
being a grown-up sucked even then.
Everyone loves a teenager.
The grandfather was there to do the forgiving.
No one remembers if any of them were fat.

But he has been born again in someone else's story.
Son, for the return home,
if we look him square in the cross-eyes,
will we recognise ourselves?
Find our fast-talking character
buried deep in the seed of his caricature,

seeds of the migrant dream still
black-faggoting their way into black rainbows.

When the factory has become a song and dance musical
and *Telesā* is an e-book best-seller, we are –
one word at a time – each an ant carrying a grain of sand on our backs,
changing the landscape into another imaginary configuration.

I grew up watching someone else's fantasy island – da plane, da plane –
aloha shirts, cocktails, golf carts, midgets.
That was a place where tourists go,
but we are writing
to return home.

I dream of you as yet unborn story,
unfolding the echo of ancients,
the source of the wild yam at your centre
feeding a French-fried generation something solid.
Ufi, yams, a whole lost world orbited around the cycle of this sacred crop,
as it made its way out of the ground,
into our mouths with the precision of a circular calendar.
We stepped back into the future,
following the counter-intuitive hands
of a truly round clock,
the past in front of us like a non-linear time-space compass ...

That life, where we once belonged,
that we know so little about, it seems stranger than fiction,
where we once followed the novel of the night sky
and the sentences in the wingspans of sky birds
felt poems in the swells of waves
by lying flat-backed on the bottom of boats ...
translated the dizzying texts of ocean movement
into the unlocked haiku
of directions.

It's not just Disney.
Even NASA is looking to the Moana,
oceanographers following Marshallese memory
to way-find beyond GPS in a post-satellite era.

Scientists are telling us our genes
are designed for
what we have
always known.

We are made for long-distance travelling.
Even if this fed to us as fat
through the language of obesity,
I imagine us
resisting the passive aggression
of an English-speaking world
that would cast us as overweight third person
in our own story.
In this digital age,
we will rise,
unborn sons for the return home,
daughters of the migrant dream,
and all those swimming in the in-between and beyond – of gender binaries,
pens in our hands, phones in our pockets, iPads on our tables, laptops on our backs,
    keyboards at our fingertips,
all the power of the protagonist,
long-distance travelling
through this world
as it has currently been imagined
into another one.

WE FIND OURSELVES STATISTICS

Facts rarely speak for themselves,
with ancestral pride and sociological imagination.
Let us ask better questions.

Let us not follow the numbers
that make us add up to
not enough.

Even numbers are rarely even.
We find ourselves on odd un-level playing fields,
where we have to high jump bar graphs,
pole vault poverty lines,
climb the bell curves
of slippery privilege
to be considered equal.

We always have a way to go.

Some days, the divides in the mind
can be too wide to straddle,
especially when widely documented,
well-established empirical track-records
of failure
are front of mind
for blindfolded professionals and institutions
who find us and forever bind us –
three-legged in every race.

It's easy to get angry
when six-figured salaried head-starts
look back and wave, full of first-place and
disdain
for the runners-up, with no idea of the hurdles,
or the funny business at the starting gate,
or the violent overthrows at the beginning
of a dehumanised race.

With short memories
and slow-burning strategies,
national standards, benchmarks,
blueprints, policy docs,
search for quick-fire quick-fixes,
and politicians land low blows
in a game where the gold has gone
to the same people for a long time.

Some days, I have entitlement envy.
But in the cheap seats, still we reach,
still believing in deconstructed dreams,
low-deciled and deprived, reaching
for the glow we see on the other side.

But we must promise ourselves
that we will never follow the numbers
down the rabbit holes of deficit,
get stuck there in a zero-sum game,
finding ourselves adding up to
the sum total of the problem.

Instead we must search
for the unseen calculations,
the minuses, the divides, the long distances,
the tiny fractions of proportions leftover,
the skinny pieces on the pie chart plate,
the disproportionate odds ratios
that explain the terrain
where we land disadvantaged feet,
but that never
adequately measures our hopes,
energy, effort, offerings or heartbeats.

With the right information,
let us find the solutions
we already know our people to be –
always so much more
than the sum of our parts.

FINDING OUR WAY

Make sure
you navigate today
with a vision
that connects you
to what really matters.

Tei iā koe rai te rapa i tō 'oe
You have the blade of your paddle,
I have the blade of mine.

New dawn breaks after new dawn.
We are still blessed to have our eyes
on this ever-changing horizon,
where satellites speak with mysterious
   tongues,
locating us with precision.

But we have always known
that knowing exactly where you are,
all of the time, isn't what is *really* worth
   knowing.

It is about the ability to find the way–
our way, your way, our way.

For we know in this new land
the Government is never our family.

Not like home,
where we are connected
by blood, neighbours,
village, church, schools,
and slim, dusty streets.

Back there,
where it would never do
to leave a chunk of society behind,
to leave part of the classroom behind,
because we are kāinga, 'aiga, family,
connected with one another.

Here, where they do not always see
that our children, too, are wholehearted.
Young people leaping off into their own lives,
sometimes with no elders
in their boats.

Io, it is true,
we do not have a generation to waste.

You have the blade of your paddle –
Tei iā koe rai te rapa i tō 'oe –
I have the blade of mine.

But what are our points of reference
when our celestial blueprints are lost
in dimly lit skies?

Polluted by light, smoke, fog, exhaust,
the remains of other people's progress agendas,
as the seas swell, as ice caps melt,
as the land shrinks.

Can we remember
the ways we expanded our islands
to the fullness of their environments?
Birds, sea, sky, coral reef; where the oceans
are our pathways to each other?

And when we find ourselves
in single-file city streets,
how do we move as a collective?

How do we find our pathways
to each other?

How do we not get lost
in the narrow corridors of state houses,
deciled and deprived?

We must make sure
that our minds
do not shrink to the size
of these rented, subdivided, sections
in suburban landscapes on the south-sides,
cut into pieces too small
for any harvest,
too small,
for dreaming feet.

Will our mamala trees grow
in these backyards?

Will we find the healing
that once grew on trees,
as far as the eye can see?

Can we search for the wild yams
and find the vine
that connects us to the source?

And if
these seeds
won't grow
in these new lands,
can we find ways to feed our families
that sustain mind, body and spirit?

Moʻui lelei e sino, ʻatamai mo e laumālie?
Can we feed what is hungry?
Can we slake the thirst of our children?

And when their bodies are tired,
when their spirits are sore,
when their bones are broken,
will we have surgeons, psychiatrists,
psychologists, niu healers
in our vaka?
Knowing that,
ʻO le fogavaʻa e tasi.
There is only one deck.

And there are those
trained to feel the swells,
the deep swells,
which we have never known
the likes of before.

One cut to the body is a cutting.
More than one cut to the body is a pattern.
Are there those among us,
trained to see these swells?
Feel the deep water currents?
Follow that underwater lightning
to where it might strike?

Are there safe hands
on our vaka
to hold these children?
For there is only one deck.

And for those
who are fearful and frightened,
can we create spaces where we say,
I lafoia i le fogavaʻa tele?
Cast it on the big deck.
Let us share in your fear and pain –
this is our cultural terrain
and there is room for you.

We don't leave anyone behind.

For you are bound to us in love.
We are bound to you in service;
we are bound to each other
in respect – faʻaaloʻalo, fakaʻapaʻapa.
We know there is only one deck.

Even if
our mamala trees won't grow
in this foreign soil,
we will plant and cultivate
the ability to relate.

We will nurture the essence
of who you are.

We will go forward into our past
and bring us back to our future.

We will grow mutual understandings.
Because remembering
who we are
and living
what that means,
in spaces and places
that constrain and contain
all we were meant to be.
The stakes are high
and it is never just 'a nice to have' –
it's about collective destiny.

And as a new generation
grows up,
understanding better
how the system works,
they will *step up*, work hard,
to make the system
work for us.

We will be
the people
that we've been called
to be.

Because
we are the ones
we've been waiting for.

OUR FEARS

(FOR FALA: A POEM FOR THE LIVING WAGE MOVEMENT AOTEAROA)

This fear
that there is not enough,
although we make enough food to feed the world
many times over.

This fear
that we are not enough,
and we buy and we buy and we buy
to keep other people's eyes on and off us.

This fear
that we are not safe
unless we have savings, insurance, stocks, bonds, assets, investment properties –
all the different kinds of ways to save for every kind of rainy day.

This fear
that there is not enough to go around
and we must stake our ground,
live within the confines of those white picket fences;
simply do our best within those boundaries.

This fear
that we must each have the largest slice of the pie possible;
that if we paid a wage high enough so that people can feed their own families
it would tip the whole pie cart over.

This fear
that these ideas are so normal to us
in the society we live in,
of pies, cakes and crumbs.

This fear
that we are not enough
to do anything about it.

MOEMOEĀ
(COMPOSED FOR POETS FOR IHUMĀTAO)

I have a dream ...
Not a Martin Luther King dream,
more of a waking life dream
where you're in a parallel universe
movie of your own making.

In my dream,
Jacinda is walking in knee-high gumboots,
the tall, skinny, expensive kind
you used to have to order from Great Britain
and that I could never pull over my big Tongan calves.
She is wearing a red, red raincoat,
not like a Kathmandu one with a zip.
It's more of a cape,
fire-truck red, lipstick-red, Labour-party-red.
More of a Red-Riding-Hood cape
and it is billowing in the whipping wind.

And the way she struts, it could be a Horse Polo ad
but it's not, cos she and her gumboots
are on the whenua at Ihumātao,
and she's not walking alone.
Flanked, either side, is Nanaia, Kiritapu, Willow-Jean
and Louisa, who has the reddest lipstick of them all.
They all have knee-high boots and red jackets,
and there is Carmel – taller than the rest –
even though her boots are flat,
who used to rent our family home.
And there is Jenny, with a red flower behind her ear,
who used to be married to my ex-husband.

And there is 'Anahila, my mate,
with her righteous Tongan afro, and Poto too.
And in my dream the soundtrack is Beyoncé playing
'Run the World (Girls)'

And behind them is Jacinda's baby-daddy
pushing Neve Te Aroha in an expensive waterproof pram,
which is just as well cos there is thunder and lightning
as these women walk.
And it strikes me that he is the perfect,
mana-ful, woke male.

The lips of all these women are pursed.
Not like in selfies, but like they are purposeful.
And in my dream, they are walking in slow-mo
and Marama is there in her reggae beanie, laughing,
saying, *what took you fellas so long*.

In my dream,
Jacinda has read Dr Rawiri Taonui's article
and as her plane landed on the Auckland tarmac
she thought for the first time
about all the bodies, all the bones, the kōiwi,
the ancestors who had to give up everything:
a clean awa, their land, kaimoana,
maunga to be quarried, ocean to become a sewer.
They who had to give too much to the city of Auckland,
even their graves.

I dream Jacinda truly felt
that this history stinks like sewage,
as she drove into the shit-show
that has been the water treatment plant.
And she visibly flinched when she saw the 1863 Proclamation

issued by corrupt Governor Grey
with his fake news about dangerous, attacking natives,
as he coveted Waikato-Tainui having the best land, flour mills, most fertile export businesses,
and imported and gathered 16,000 British imperial and colonial troops,
telling the natives to surrender,
or they'd be ejected.

I hope she knows
the archaeologists say
this is an OG settlement place.
Where to quote Alice Te Punga Somerville,
where Māori
'Once were Pacific'
and evolved, over centuries,
right here,
from us
into them.
And I'm waving a Tongan flag
at this small way that we are connected,
and in my dream,
Pita Turei is not comparing me to Captain Cook
for doing this, but he's down there on the atea
saying 'haere mai Jacinda',
and he looks so beautiful,
with his feathers in his hair.

And in my dream, at this very moment,
he turns into a bird
and then he is joined by an army of kāhu
from Okahu Bay,
a whole field full of black hawks
with surveyor's pegs in their beaks
and a burning papa kainga in their eyes.
And yeah, maybe a park for all New Zealanders

is not enough, although it was gifted generously after the occupation of Bastion Point.
And there are overlapping interests here,
not just the fact that blood joins
in so many mokopuna,
but cos the kaupapa of Tino Rangatiratanga
is an overlapping interest.
And even Paul Majurey says, *tautoko*.

And then all the maunga are there
cos Pihanga led the way,
and just like Pania,
she's quite the mountain.
It's Mana Wāhine on display
and there's the red line-up of women
walking in the mud
and I don't know where Willie, Kelvin and Peeni are,
but it's my dream and I don't need to know.
Willie is def not doing the fingers at the crowd
behind the glass doors at Parliament, like I saw him do last week.
Just cos men who have had their children taken by the state heckled him.

And to be honest
I'm sure uplift kaupapa is over.
It's time for uplifting.

And in my dream, all the boots on those women
are now thigh-high and they are all wearing
ei katu of red flowers
made by my friend Taʻi,
cos it's Cook Islands language week
and cos every woman looks more beautiful in an ei.
Everyone.
And they are saying *Kia Ora, Kia Orana*.

And I am looking at Pania, Qiane, Amiria and the cousins.
Rihanna is singing, shining bright, bright like a diamond,
but not a blood diamond.
And Qiane says: 'We don't speak on behalf of Mana Whenua. We are Mana Whenua.'
And there is a sign in the sky,
not a tōhu but a billboard,
and it says,
'Aotearoa, New Zealand. This LEADERSHIP is in dispute.'
And there are one hundred thousand likes on Facebook
and laughing, dancing GIFS and
emojis with love hearts in their eyes.

And then suddenly it is silent,
and in my dream Jacinda stops
and takes off her gumboots
and is barefoot, skin to land,
and tears stream down her face
and she says, *I can hear it*,
I can feel the whenua singing.

Once you know it,
you cannot unknow it.

We do not hurt the things we love.

And in amidst that magic,
somewhere online,
a give-a-little page
has gone viral
and people are buying back
Ihumātao, square metre by square metre,
and the soundtrack is playing 'Midnight Oil',
and the donations pour in.
Asians for Tino Rangatiratanga,

the Muslim community,
the Tongan church congregations
who give more than they can afford
because that's how we roll,
and the amounts are printed online,
and even Don Brash donates because,
no he doesn't, because not even in a dream!
But nobody cares,
because he is old news
and now girls rule the world.

And Jacinda stands up and says
to the international community

This is a win for climate change. This is a win for indigenous people everywhere.

This is a win for community. This is a win for New Zealand.

This is a win for Auckland. This is a win for the whenua.

The soundtrack is playing 'The People'
by Louis Baker.

And even Tina Ngata says,
she did better than Helen Clark.

And on TV,
beautiful Kanoa Lloyd,
rapturous in red,
sits there,
queen of the Prime Time universe,
and with a smug side-eye at her colleagues,
she interviews Joe Bloggs
from the heart of Remuera

about why he gave a little
and then he explains
that after coming to the whenua himself
and taking the tour with Pania
and reading about the history
he finally understood
that the people of Ihumātao
had given enough
to make Auckland great.

And it was time to stop taking.

Or living off the back of benefits
of unjustly taken land.

It was time to give a little back.
He said, *Actually, it is time*
to give a lot.

And somewhere
in Tāmaki,
all the birds waiting
with surveyor pegs
in their mouths,
both extinct and living,
spat them from the
choke in their throats
and the black hawks
began to sing.

And all the people everywhere,
who can hear the dawn chorus of the dead,
locked in psychatric wards and prison cells,
began to hum a happier tune
instead of feeling lament.

And somewhere,
Te Whiti, Tōhu, Te Kooti, Rua, Rewi, Tāwhiao,
Eva, Whina, Ngāneko and all the ancestors,
began to sing.
Knowing now,
the tongues of birds.

And us ordinary ones,
without the gifts of sight or sound,
if you listen carefully
you can catch a fragment
of that waiata,
you can hear it
in the refrain of
Rob Ruha's new song,
and it
sounds like

freedom.

A TONGAN REFLECTION ON TINO RANGATIRATANGA

I remember I used to feel
shame
when someone made fun of my king:
'Knickerbockers
Aping European royalty,'
they said.
The heavy crowns
on sweating, brown brows.
The ermine trimming
in stifling heat.
The titles of chamberlain
barons and nobles.
I used to
feel
shame.
I did not realise
at the time,
the power
of mimic
as a strategy
of resistance.
The power of
forcing someone
to recognise power
because
it is wearing the same clothes
and has a written constitution.

I did not realise the power
of forcing power
to see power,
instead of savages
ripe for the colonising.

Even today,
it is illegal for a Tongan
to walk shirtless
in public.
The paranoia
of King George the first.
The genuine worry
that foreign ships
would land;
take things into
their own hands.
Put down their flag.
Take over.

As preposterous as it now seems,
then, it was the
done thing.
A King who
was fully tattooed,
[legend has it,
EVERYWHERE

on his body]
who outlawed tatau,
wiped it out
in one generation
to secure
an image,
to keep us
secure.

I did not realise
that it was a strategy –
erasing structures and symbols
seen as savage,
appropriating structures and symbols
power could recognise
as power.

Now when
there is some
snide remark
about coronations
or knickerbockers
or 'kings' in inverted commas
or lower case caps,
I wonder
what they
would prefer.
A King who serves
cocktails in an island shirt,
plays the ukulele
on a fantasy island,
'da plane, da plane, da plane'
ensures the guest houses
are air conditioned,

serves sashimi
with fresh mango,
with girls in grass skirts
swaying,
coconut bras
'come and eat'
'relax'
'take a load off'
'welcome to paradise'
'come for a ride on my royal golf cart'...
Would that
be more to your liking?
Piss off
with what you think
our leadership
should be like.

For all of its faults,
this is
tino rangatiratanga.
Manifest
by hook
or by crook,
by copycat
or mimic –
the knickerbockers
are part of how
we resisted you.

Shame.

TŪHOE BOYS

I said to my mate,
I'm going to write an ode
to Tūhoe boys.

She said, Don't.

But I've never been good
at doing what I'm told.

I think maybe
Tūhoe are the Tongans
of Aotearoa.

The way that Ngāti Porou
are the Samoans,
Te Arawa are the Cookies,
and Ngāpuhi are the Niueans.

I get myself in trouble
for saying racist things like this.

But it would explain my attraction.

A Tūhoe boy I once knew
said that instead of
flash oratory
on the marae,
he set the bait traps
in the forest.

That was his ritual.
I was impressed,
Even though I love me
a good whaikōrero.

A Tūhoe boy I once knew
said after the revolution
and there was tino rangatiratanga
everywhere
he wanted to know,
what we would eat for breakfast.

Then he set about decolonising
his diet, bypassing the supermarket
getting his milk
directly from a cow
growing his own green
making his own cheese

walking the talk
cooking the cook
eating the eat.
I thought maybe
he was the man for me.
But he didn't agree.

That's ok
Because you can lead a horse
to water,
but if you can force them to drink
they aren't a Tūhoe boy.

Maybe I like them
cos they tend to be short
but they can fill up a room
with jokes, and story, and ihi and wehi
in the way that they become a mountain
and every other man
stands
in their shadow.

This would be too much
If they weren't schooled
in the fine art
of self-depreciation.

I like this in a man.

A Tūhoe boy I once knew
in his mid-sixties,
once blew off facilitating a panel
at a conference,
because he wanted to keep on
talking to me.

I like my men like that.
A bit rogue.
Kind of rude.
Fucking charming.

A Tūhoe boy I once knew
was all nervous shimmer in a room.
Whenever you looked at him
he wasn't looking.
I knew he was watching.
Everything.
I could feel it.
and he could feel it back.

You gotta be careful of those ones.
They'll catch your interest
with a story not meant for you
but meant for you,
a buck each way.

I'm a sucker
For a gambling man
who can carefully
calculate the odds
otherwise known
as cheating.

I'm the daughter of one,
Maybe my dad
is the most Tūhoe Tongan
you could ever meet.

I once knew a Tūhoe boy
who said poetry was his job.

He called waiata song-poetry
and haka dance-poetry.

Then quoted some Pākehā academic
pretended he couldn't remember
her name
and couldn't pronounce it.
He asked for help,
Her name fell off my lips.
That cunning dumb,
in the name of trying to catch
how clever you are.

They don't give a shit
about first impressions
it's all about them sussing
whether you are a dick or not.

Us Tongans do that too.
It's called fie-vale-loi.
this translates
'wanting to be stupid: lying.'

I know that game.

Bluster, bluff, buffoon,
all in the name of
I don't give a shit
but, actually, I do.

I once knew a Tūhoe boy
who could see dead people.
I find that kind of thing attractive.

Which may be why I'm still single.

One day
I might meet a short mountain
named after a tupuna
who can tell good jokes
write dance-poems and song-poems
wring the necks
of his own free-range chickens
feed me sweet, happy eggs on toast
and make a self-composting toilet
to protect the mauri of his ancestor
the river.

I might
make him mine
for a moment,
before he returns
to the mist.

Maybe.

FOR TAMIR, WITH LOVE FROM AOTEAROA

Tamir Rice,
let me apologise.
I cannot begin the day
with reading any more
about you.
I know your killers
were set free.
What am I to do
but feel hopeless tears
fall in my coffee
first thing?
Know that I name you,
Tamir Rice.
I see your beautiful smile.
I have no words
for the perpetrators
who have killed dreams
like so many before them.
My words are for you.
Know that I see your face
in my sons',
but not their fate.

In this country,
racism is not
so trigger happy
but it is still uniformed.
Here, young men
who look like my sons
are more likely
to be imprisoned
than anyone else
in the world.
In the world, Tamir.
Our police force
admits to unconscious bias.
But you are not
unconscious Tamir.
You are dead, child,
and it is here our grief rests.
All of that freedom lost,
living or dead.

All of that control,
which in its zenith
becomes
life or death.
It is for all of that fear and hatred
whereby
some people
are dehumanised
to the point
that they become
visible threats,
moving targets,
just
by being
in their own bodies.
We know that on some level
they will try
and defame you
and blame you,
like all the other innocents
they kill in cold blood.
There is a certain kind of history
that leads us here, Tamir,
that they do not teach in schools.

It is a long legacy,
centuries of life-taking,
land-stealing, plunder
of resources, diamonds,
coal, forests, farms, water,
everything, taken by
organised
mass-murder.
Know Tamir, that this happened
almost all over the world.
Whole countries were taken.
Whole peoples were wiped out,
many enslaved,
ways of living
and languages were
stopped, not lost,
at the ends of guns.
At the end of brutal wars
that were not
sought out
by the innocents
nor evenly matched.
The casualties of
that level of violence
brutality and abuse,
of technology,
weaponry and power,
cannot even be counted.

When you descend
from the perpetrators
of that kind of atrocity
and you live on the land
you have taken by force,
when your whole empire
is built on the benefits
of what has been
paid for by innocent blood,
it triggers a deep fear,
and sometimes
unconscious bias
makes you protect
your power at gunpoint.
Police, the prizes of that plunder,
whether you realise it or not,
it's hard to feel safe
in your own fair skin,
instinctively protecting others
who share
in that privilege.
There is deep fear
of retaliation, retribution,
or simply – and most often –
reciprocity.
Anyone that has reason to rise up.
It makes them try and control things in
crazy ways, Tamir,
especially the stories
of who they were and who they are,
especially the stories
of who we were and who we are.
You cannot believe their stories Tamir,
or you would think that killing a child
and walking free
is legitimate.
Tamir, the things
they have to tell themselves
so that they can sleep at night.
The lies they have to tell their children.
The spiritual stories they have to tell
  about themselves
to justify mass murder,
thievery on an epic scale.
The way they have to twist even the bible
and definitions of who is
and who is not
a neighbour
that you have to love
as thyself.
Their religion, their history, their holidays
of thanksgiving and other epic mistruths;
slanted stories of discovering 'new lands' –
they teach it as truth, Tamir.

There is a deep denial of reality, Tamir.
The things they have to hide, Tamir.
The deep fear
under it all.
The children
they still
have to kill,
who are casualties
of them policing
their privilege.
None of this is new
but I want to say to you,
it is because of all of this
that you are
no longer a
breathing
child.
All of it
is embodied
fresh
in your dead body,
child.

We remember you
as one of the fallen,
following
in the lost footsteps
of so many
good people
who have gone
before you.
I imagine them greeting you –
old souls, kindred spirits –
with the angels who watch
over those
who succumb
to such hatred.
Tamir,
know that we ache.
We, who know the difference
between right and wrong,
good and evil,
between a child
and a moving target.
We know why
they kill
our children,
and in honouring our dead,
we will never
give up
on creating a world
in which you would have
lived.

NOW THIS IS REVERSE RACISM

This is what we say amongst ourselves.
That many of you, if not most of you,
(if not her specifically, or him, definitely, him)
needs a good screw!
And we laugh, laugh, laugh
about the fact that you're not getting any
and how it clearly informs
so much of what you do!

It's why you're so mean.
It's why you're so cold.
It's why you don't make eye contact with people you don't know.
It's why your grim smiles don't reach your eyes.
Why you are so polite without being friendly.
It's why you build roads in straight lines
that do not lead us to each other.
Straight lines like the Great South Road –
a forgotten former war path;
a roadway of Empire;
a trail of death.

It's why there is poetry in your prose,
no oratory in your explanations,
no art in your science.
It's why your conversations are always
heading in straight lines –
no room for a garden, the indirect path,
the deep ocean road where things are left unsaid
in the still waters between us.
Silence that can be translated in twenty different ways.
Just straight lines that go nowhere –
ambiguous.

These are the things we say among ourselves.
It's why your laughter never reaches
past your throat,
into your lungs,
through your body,
reverberating out into the va.

It's why your eyes are empty
and no one's home.
Cos you're worrying about your:
mortgage, taxes, salary scale,
the property values, interest rates,
underclass, GDP, OECD, and how
we're slipping ... the sustainability of the economy,
whether we are worth talking to, and oh,
what do you do for a living?

It's why your eyes are empty
and no one's home
to respond
to the living, breathing, humans around you.

You are indifferent, absent, elsewhere.
Anywhere but present,
eyes open,
closed heart.

It's why you put your old folks
in old folks' homes.
It's why you contract out the caring
of your babies; no cuddling is allowed
in your kindergartens; qualifications are required
to nurture children in nests with locked gates.
It's why you uniform your young people

and your world is full of bells and
alarm clocks, time sheets, pay checks,
meetings that start on time, without prayers,
and end without ritual or song.

We know, like Maya, why the caged bird
sings, or loses its voice,
or starves itself in an economy of abundance.
We know why the old people lose their minds
before their time, dementia marbles rolling
in institutional hallways,
along miles of linoleum that
smells bad and goes nowhere.
That lives in the floors in
lunatic asylums and prisons and all
of the places where the caged birds don't sing
and get done in, bright feathers in hospital pajamas,
electronic convulsive therapy for bird-brains,
thieving fingers behind bars,
psychos in solitary confinement,
or locked in hospital beds.

And they are never touched,
or sung to,
or massaged,
with warm, oiled hands,
sending the ghosts to rest.
And visiting hours are at the end
of long, lonely motorways of days
that blend into dead ends
and die in council flats, unnoticed.
The sky is always locked out in those places.
People can't see the blue, blue of ever-changing sky
and the people inside

never laugh, laugh, laugh
like the sun breaking through cloud,
never sing, sing, sing
like the leaves in the wind,
never pick flowers,
spending hours,
weaving them into garlands
for a lei
that will last
one
day.

Who never catch anything fresh
from the ocean and eat it
raw,
with awe.

Who don't take time
to squeeze the unctuous oil from nuts
so you can run fingers over glossy skin

and SIN,

or warm and shape the bodies
of young children from birth, from babies,
who grow up, muscles massaged and skin sweet,
held and warm, sleeping in Mother's bed, in Grandmother's bed …
who never sleep alone.

You, who never sleep with babies
but instead build cots
of walled bars for your infants,
teach them to self-soothe,
to feed and piss and shit on a timetable,

to love their routine,
and suck plastic nipples into the dark, cold nights,
and drink powdered milk
from the breasts of goats or cows,
or soya protein with added emulsifiers.

We chew food for the next generation in our mouths,
scoop it out with clean fingers
into little gums,
the small mouths of babies born from our bodies,
transferring spit
and sustenance
and spirit.

We are told by Plunket nurses
we are unhygienic.

We are told by the coroners,
don't sleep with your babies.

We are told ... well, our ears are filled
with your waxing and waning about us ...

but when we are amongst ourselves ...
out of your earshot ...
these are the kinds of things
We say ABOUT THEM.

FOR ALL MY SISTERS
(FOR B)

I imagine that part of her
remembers being bird.

Birds are the dinosaurs
that survived the meteorite,

that found their wings
in all that fire.

                                                      I imagine
                                                      the bird part of you

                                                      in your muscle memory,
                                                      or buried elegantly
                                                      in your skeletal structure

                                                      would have risen up
                                                      in shock,

                                                      out of your body,

                                                      flown far away
                                                      somewhere safe.

Even today

I watch you flutter
in and out
of conversation,

disassociation,
they call it,

where you go

I do not want to know.

Somewhere blue-nested
I hope,
sky and cloud.

Nowhere near
memory:
breath, body fluids,
hands, genitals, saliva, spit
or semen.

                                        I wish you all kinds
                                        of wings,
                                        little sister.

                                        Wings as wide
                                        as the Pterosaurs.

                                        Wings as dark
                                        as flying foxes.

                                        Wings as white
                                        as a heron.

Not everything
happens for a reason.

Some things
are not supposed
to be life lessons,

or challenges to overcome,

or growth experiences.

Some things
can only be carried.

Some things
cannot be explained: *rape culture,   masculinity*
cannot be explained, *entitlement,   patriarchy*
cannot be explained, *objectification,   dehumanising*
cannot be explained, *domination,   power*
cannot be explained, *perversion,   sexual addiction*
cannot be explained, *lust,   desire*
cannot be explained, *victim   becomes perpetrator*
cannot be explained, *abused,   damaged*
CANNOT be explained away.

This shit
should not
have happened
to you.

Who asked for it?
The girl in the short skirt?
Who asked for it?
The daughter who grew breasts?
Who asked for it?
The wife who didn't know her place?
Who asked for it?
The granddaughter who trusted him to sit on his lap?
Who asked for it?
The niece who grew up too fast?
Who asked for it?
The girl who accepted a ride home in your car?
Who asked for it?
Your colleague who got drunk at the party?

Who asked for it?
The flirt who walked home by herself?
Who asked for it?
The woman who bared her arms?
Who asked for it?
The woman in her own home minding her own business?
Who asked for it?
Who asked for it?
Who asked for it?

    No one did.
    That's the point.
    No one.

    And now
    you are
    sisters
    living
    with
    straw men.

I wish you a spinning wheel
that can turn straw into gold.
I wish you a fairy godmother.
I wish you magical red shoes.
I wish you a white handkerchief
with three drops of
your dead mother's blood.
I wish you an Excalibur sword.
I wish you a dangerous dragon.
I wish you a tall tower.
I wish you a magic mirror
that would say
oh how beautiful you are,
the fairest of them all.

I wish it was just
a fairytale.
Just a bad story
with a sick,
unexpected
twist.

If I could build you
a safe house
where he could huff
and puff
but not
blow your house in,
I would.

But he's been there.
He's been everywhere.
He's been inside.

I wish you wings
little sister.
And claws.
I wish you tooth
and nail.
And armour
and chainmail.
And forks
and knives.
I wish you
guns and tanks
and an eye
for an eye.
I wish you bricks
and sticks
and stones.

I wish you
everything

and everyone

you needed

and wasn't

there

when you

needed it.

I wish you
the grace
to forgive us.

I wish you
the power
to rise
from the ashes
in your eyes,
but if
the mythological
bird
doesn't
work for you,
I wish you more matches.
I wish you fire.

If only memories
could burn.

Some things
can only be carried.

I wish you the strength
and mana

to carry
what you need to.

And if you can
let it go,
and you choose to,

let it be carried away
by a fast-running stream,

let it be washed away
by salty, warm waves,

let it be buried in the softest earth,

let it be whispered into the trunk of a tree
and held there for safe-keeping.

But if you want to use
what happened
to wound back,

speak truth to power,

to expose,
to hold to account,
to strip,
to imprison,

then let me be by your side
with popcorn
and movies
and self-help books
and chocolate
and tissues.

Let me create a safe space
between us
with listening ears
and loving eyes.

Let me create a safe space
and a safe bed
in my house,
open twenty-four hours.

Let me create a safe family.

Let me create safe sons.

Let me create a safe community.

Let me create safe workplaces.

Let me create a safe culture.

Let me create a safe digital, virtual world.

Let me create a safe society.

Let us take back the night.

Let us take back the bedroom.

Let us take back the back seat of the car.

Let us take back what it means to be drunk.

Let us take back what it means to be a date.

Let us take back what it means to be a girlfriend.

Let us take back what it means to be a wife.

Let us take back what it means to be a niece.

Let us take back what it means to be a sister.

Let us take back what it means to be a daughter.

Let us take back what it means to be a granddaughter.

Let us take back what it means to be a woman.

Let us take back what it means to be a girl.

**Let us begin
with that.**

LOST

AND
FOUND

THE SOUNDS OF PRINCESS ASHIKA

The sound of tents flapping for seventeen nights outside the Shipping Corporation of Polynesia,
a vigil, a camp of families waiting in the dark,
night after night, despair tempered
by hymns and prayer.

                    The sound of more than one hundred thousand offerings:
                            tears, sweat, still sticky on those local notes,
                                    pieces of paper floating.

The sound of mourners
breaking the backs of small boats,
barely able to hold their grief above sea-level,
small boats groaning under the weight of their burden.

                    The sound of photographs silent, sombre,
                        loved ones held with trembling hands,
                  faces on T-shirts smiling lifelessly back at us.

The sound of koloa dropping into the ocean
the ngatu, the wreaths, the fine mats
the flowers, the petalled synthetic
kissing the surface of the sea,
swirling sacrifices.

> The sound of the memorial stone,
> coffin-shaped, heavy with names tapped into its back,
> tapped like tatau,
> blood, the flesh, the stain of human names on marble,
> a coffin wrapped and dropped into the water.

Oiaue. The sound of live bodies jumping into the ocean,
submerging themselves in grief,
throwing their bodies to the elements.

> But they are lost to the lost,
> irredeemably buoyant, they rise floating,
> hopelessly alive.

We all dream that our mouths are filled with the ocean,
salt at the back of our throats,
but how hopelessly afloat we are.
We all rise for another day.

> How alive we are –
> this we know for one unsettling moment –
> how alive.

In Suva, at the Patterson Mansion on Raisara Road,
the SUVs line up for another night of drinks.
It is their destiny to forever be
as is, where is, and nothing more,
whisky flowing like a swell
all the way out to the shore.

> From the Shipping Corporation of Polynesia
> we hear the bitter salt sound of 'no comment'.
> And the government that paid for the *Princess*
> will keep on paying,
> keep on paying.

And the King leaves the Kingdom
to attend a military tattoo,
drumming some kind of incessant beat,
rum-pa-pa-pam, rum-pa-pa-pam,
whisking, frisking, beating,
batting, tapping, scratching
in his ears – the bagpipes serenade him.
But can he hear the sounds of *Princess Ashika?*

                        Of seventy-four lost, of the two-month-old, the one-year-old,
                        the three two-year-olds, the three-year-olds, the four-year-old,
                        the two five-year-olds, the six-year-old, the seven-year-old,
                        the two nine-year-olds – this unnatural silence.

Only the stars were watching
when the *Princess* went down,
witness in that night sky.
Their mouths taped for the inquiry.
The silence of no comment,
Seventy-four lives lost.

                        The sound of despair tempered
                              by hymns and prayer.

SPIRITED LEADERSHIP

(FOR LOUISE AND LEADERSHIP NEW ZEALAND)

Let us navigate today,
open-hearted
with a spirit of inquiry,
leaving our judges behind,
embracing the archetype
of the learner.
We have learned that leadership
is not about putting more on,
but about taking stuff off.
Letting go
of what we've accumulated
that no longer serves us.
Daring to be bare.
Sometimes being naked
is your only protection from life.
Stripping the layers away
to find the puutake within,
the taproot, where we draw energy
to sustain us going forward.

Let us navigate today,
with aroha and hope for the future.
Let us heal ourselves,
in the land itself,
in the saltwater of our seas,
in the green of our forests.
Let us wash ourselves clean.

Let us create practices of care
so that we can prepare
for the hard journeys,
the lonely ones,
that involve standing on chairs
and seeing the long view,
the distant view,
the storms brewing on far shores.
Let us step up, stand up
and look at that view from that mountain,
for all those who are too busy simply
    surviving,
heads down in the engine rooms,
too busy trying to stay afloat.
Let us be bold enough to look up
beyond their horizons.
Let us resist the lure to be passengers,
to cruise, or to follow
the seductive sirens
singing their songs of private good.
Let us follow the call to what is shared,
knowing that decision-making
can be fraught with danger –
the winds can change,
the course can be perilous,
but wondering,
always wondering,
how do we find a way
through this?
Insight is the journey.

Let us navigate today
with strength of self.
Let us work out what we will take bullets for.
Let us practise our passions.
Let us not be good.
Because we do not want to navigate
the narrower lives,
tiptoe the tight-ropes of expectation,
the fine lines of perfection,
but instead, we want to be whole,
aware of our shadows
that loom long over our decks.
Let us take the time to look.
Let us hold on to our discomfort
for long enough
to know what it means.
Let us be responsible
for our own inner culture,
knowing that what is within
is so often without.

Let us navigate today with purpose.
Let us not be
consumed by the urgent,
the reactive, the risk-averse,
the bland leading the bland,
the business as usual.
Let us get off the auto-cue queue.
Let us be the ones who take risks
in service of a greater vision,
knowing that we cannot control outcomes
but we can understand the causal chains
that inform our intervention logic:
open to doubt,

encountering the unknown,
avoiding amygdala hijacks
of shame, fear and blame
rooted deeply in our psyches.
Let us hold onto our uncertainty
and our potential vastness –
tap the taproot,
stand in our power
with awareness.

Let us navigate today
in a spirit of manaakitanga,
embracing diversity.
Let us be open to disagreement
without attachment,
knowing that
when everyone thinks the same,
no one is thinking.
Let us be open to being challenged
and see where we are triggered.
Let us communicate with people
in ways that they can hear.
Let us temper what we are good at.
Let us know what is 'me'
and what is not 'them'.
Let us walk in their jandals.
Let us be able to influence others
who think differently from us,
but let us listen
with our hearts
and not know the other
in ways that render them
done and dusted.
Let us remember

that it takes less energy
to stick with our own biases.
Let us find the levers in diversity
and be prepared to disagree,
experiencing the fullness of reality
through other people's perspectives.

Let us navigate today with courage
and when we find that we are
digging ourselves deeper
into holes
of our own making,
let us be brave enough
to put down the spade
and call it:
the spade the spade.
Let us dare to be disruptive.
Let us be wise
about what we are dependent upon.
Let us be bold enough
to rethink a system
that sends our waste
into our rivers that are life-giving.
Let us disinvest
in what one day will destroy us.
Let our values
consciously underpin the bricks and
mortar we build
in our designs for life.
Let us use our knowledge
to navigate a finite world.
Let us thrive in a world with limits.
Let us be the people
who just went and built the bloody thing

until other people 'turned up'.
Let us get our gumboots on;
let us nut it out for all of us.

Let us navigate today in a spirit of unity.
Let us up our conversations
about what matters,
find the levers of change,
contribute to collective wisdom,
creative thinking, consciousness,
but let us have a broader vision
that catches the periphery and rear-view
that can bear to see
who benefits
from our leadership
and who benefits
by the smallness of our groups
and who doesn't.

Let everyone on this waka
know that they are welcome guests.
Let us believe passionately
that people can do a lot more
than they think.
Let us create environments
in our circles of influence,
where people feel empowered enough
to make something happen.
Let us harness the institutions
we are a part of
to enable these visions.
Let us stand in our power
with awareness.

Let us navigate today with the long view,
Let us have a 150-year-long strategic plan,
be the ones who invest in the technology
that prepares us for the unexpected,
who design the tramways,
who add value to the milk,
who add milk to the diets
of the next generation,
stretching beyond the short-term
and the self-interest.
Let us plant trees with strong roots
in anticipation of those brewing storms
on the changing climate of the far horizon,
so that the land holds,
so that the land holds,
and the people prosper
when it hits our shores.

Let us navigate today,
embracing and open-hearted.
Let us take everyone with us.
Let us never forget where we come from.
Let us be humble,
knowing that we walk in the paths
other people have carved
with their bullshit odometers on,
asking themselves, is it true, is it really true
that we cannot do this?
Let us take responsibility for our conscience,
knowing that others might walk in the trails
that we leave behind.
Or lack a trail,
because we were not
courageous enough

to bushwhack them,
to walk them,
or to make them wide enough
so that we can move as a collective.

Let us be those leaders
who beat the drums,
orchestrate drama, dance, theatre,
and sing songs of the sea
in all sorts of strange languages
that ache with purpose, passion and
possibility
and inspire the next generation
to build boats
that will carry them into the future,
navigating wisely,
with courage, unity, spirit, purpose,
strength of self, manaakitanga,
hope for the future, aroha,
open-hearted,
with the long view,
with a spirit of inquiry.

Let us be those leaders
who operate in ways
so that people barely know
that we were trying to lead them –
so that they will say:
we did it ourselves.

LOST AND FOUND

(FOR GARRY GOTTFRIEDSON
– KAMLOOPS CANADA)

We've entered this strange forest
without our stories.
Enchanted suburbs, surreal streets,
   fabled fences –
the thrones of private properties;
the dense darkness
of rentals and real estate.

It is someone else's fairy tale.

What was once alive and thriving
all around us, in all of its wildness,
is numbed and
concrete dumbed
down to pedicured,
manicured,
houseware accessory,
asphyxiated under asphalt,
fenced and white picketed,
trimmed and chopped
within an inch
of its wild life.

What was once natural
has been reframed
as natural resource,
to be mined
for all its worth.

Unrecognisable
to us
as even
alive.

Let alone for us to remember
that we are relatives,
born of the same universe.

Empire
dismissed our worldviews,
unearthed us from our language,
replaced it with the tongues of trade –
the etymology of Empire.

We found ourselves dictated to by a language
that names all else as foreign –
a Queenly mother-tongue
that beat itself into a thousand tiny mouths
with whips and straps, punishment and slaps.
A language
that names the world
and knows it all.

This language is
all I have to offer you.
Even as I speak through it,
it knows me.

We've entered this strange forest
without knowing the rituals
to keep us safe.

We've entered this forest,
no stories to guide us,
to tell us where we are.
No elder to interpret for us
the language of birds,
cloud, wind, moving grasses, insects.

We've entered this forest,
where the only narratives we inherit
are theirs.
We are already the baddies.
We are Indians – savages
of the south seas.
They are in the cowboy hats,
captains of great ships,
spinning silver pistols,

the honour of armed forces, armadas.
Keeping everyone
safe
from us.

We are all the ooga-booga
they can imagine.
Unholy, heathen, dirty,
brown-skinned, red-skinned,
   black-skinned, yellow-skinned.
We are off-white in some way
and it will be a problem.

Oh we've entered this strange forest
where we are not safe
because of the colour of our skins
and the dangers that lurk
in the whiteness of its dark.

We've entered this dark forest
without knowing the names
of the spirits
that have always roamed these roads.
We are left with new names,
Tina Fontaine.
New spirits
of the missing and murdered
who watch over us,
in the birds.

Not guilty
says the same nameless,
faceless people that have
made nameless, faceless decisions

that have resulted in death
for decades; resulted in unjust justice
for centuries now.

Not guilty, they say.

I say.
What is it that you are not guilty of?

But I am a visitor here
and it is fresh angry,
not the fatigued rage
that one swallows every day,
bitter pills
too pathological
to swallow –
it would make anyone
sick.

Not guilty.

Gerald Stanley,
what are you
and a jury of your peers
not guilty of?

There is never any winner in a case like this,
said the Crown Prosecutor, Bill Burge,
as a killer walked free. Winning.

We've entered this forest
so far from the
already interpreted path,
our parents can only point to

books in English they cannot read,
full of laws that sentence
us.

There is no time for stories that might
   keep us safe
after the late-shift of the second job.

In there,
somewhere,
in the oldest,
most beloved stories
of them all,
are the directions.

We re-search.

It is in a book
out of print
found in the library stack
held on another campus –
ordered,
waited for,
received.

A proverb
passed down
from one mouth to another
over centuries,
carried, remembered,
recited, related.
It breathes to me
unspoken
in the silence

of black typeset
translated into English
from beyond.

O le gase a ala lalavao.
Enunciates with breath
of ancestor,
spoken in my awkward
English accent.

I say it so slowly
but it will not roll
off my tongue.

O le gase a ala lalavao.
My accent is crap.

Brother Herman
has translated it for me –
rendered it intelligible.

The shade of high trees
will not allow the scrub
to cover your path.

The high trees
are ancestors,
always watching,
always overlooking,
ever-present,
ensuring
you find
the pathway
back to yourself.

Yes, they say,
ache in their falling leaves,
in tongues we cannot translate easily,
they say
you will find
your pathway
back to us.

We will never leave you.

The further you pull the bow back,
the farther it will reach.

POEM FOR THE COMMONWEALTH, 2018

We gather here
and feel the weight of the world
on our shoulders.

It does not feel like
we've inherited
commonwealth,
but rather,
common problems.

If we are to heed the words of poets,
Ben Okri said yesterday,
'We have entered the garden
of nightmares and wonders.
The giants have woken
and they are stirring.
We need to be roused
from the beauty
of our sleep.'

Indeed, we've entered this
strange garden
in this city,
epicentre of epitaph,
epitome of empire.

The stones in the squares
remind us
that we all died for this.
The war memorials murmur
numbers, not names.

We bring our dead with us
and they are already here.

Not just the ones marked by marble,
but our ancestors,
the original inhabitants
of the lands 'discovered'.
Who lie in the unmarked graves

and unmentioned massacres,
in battles unspoken of
in untaught wars.

We carry them like stones
in our bodies.

They too contribute
towards this commonwealth.

They gave more
than they should have.

Commonwealth.
We come with twinned sides
of the same story.
Either trauma or gain.
Both of it pain.
Two sides
of the same coin,
heads or tails –
the head is the same
on most of our money.

The commonwealth.
Some days
it does not feel like riches,

although we gather
to speak
of fairer futures.
Truth be told,
it is the fear of future
that we have most in common.

I did not come to sing a siren song
on the sinking ship of empire.
I come to sing of sinking islands
in the South Pacific,
on the blue continent
where I come from.

What is at stake
is the very land we stand on.
The earth itself rejects us.
It reneges its responsibilities.
It has retreated
back into the deep.

And if the ocean could speak
in that choked, overheated throat
gagged with plastic bags,
in the way she once spoke to us,
and we could listen,
she would say,
too much salt on her tongue,
she would say,
rising with a surety
which we have never seen before,
she would say,
ENOUGH!

If ever we needed
to wake from our sleep
and hear the call of the commonwealth,
it is now.

The islands of Oceania: Kiribati, Tuvalu,
  Samoa, Tonga, Vanuatu.

We are the canaries
in the coal mines of climate change
singing and ringing the unruly bells
beating the big drums
and yet,
drowned
out.

So here we gather,
the call of the commonwealth,
but it is the uncommon wealth
that may save us all.

Almost completely silenced,
schooled out of us,
in lost languages
that were beaten
out of the mouths of children.
There lie the answers
in cultures that hold a
wealth of knowledge,
intergenerational meditations
on what it means to be alive,
what it means to survive
in a certain set of conditions,
specific parameters of earth and sea and sky.
Each of us
holding a long-gestated
piece of the puzzle,
of how to be human and thrive.

It is a precious, peopled offering.

It is here, in the ruins of our histories,
in what is left of us, in what we have fought for,
Ka whawhai tonu matou ake ake ake,
alongside our ongoing innovation –
there lies the most precious offerings
to the commonwealth.
It is the heart of who we are,
how we see the world to be –
our richest offering.

Let us share.

My people have always known
that we are all relatives,
common ancestors,
the same stardust
in all of our bones,
the rocks, the trees, the leaves –
all of these,
our relatives, all of us –
part of the family of things.

One ancestral word at a time,
we are salvaging what has been savaged.
These backward ways
of being in the world
that may take us forward.
That wake us up
to all that we are dependent upon.
That open our eyes
as the giants sleep.

Science seems to take such a long time
to catch up.

Richard Dawkins, the evolutionary biologist,
can confirm
that the lettuce is our distant cousin.
But the stories we live by
have not changed.

If we were truly to reorient
to life as relatives,
commonwealth
would mean more
than what we might cling to
in the face of a dangerous
and uncertain future.

Let us not
use the word 'commonwealth'
to try and insulate fate
with the soft fur of fine-feathered friends.

No,
let us spread our wings
to a much wider vision than that.
It may be the end of the world as we know it
but let us not fear
the remaking of another one.

To the young people I say,
there may be no jobs
but there is plenty of work to be done.

So let us harness our collective wisdoms:
diverse, different and divergent.
Let us create an atmosphere
of kindness and love

for even the air we breathe,
fresh water, trees, people, ocean.
Let us create a dream house,
a great place to raise a family.

For therein lies the fate
of an extraordinary family of relatives.

Where what we have in common
is all of us.

KAPIHE'S PROPHESY
(WITH GRATITUDE TO MANULANI ALULI MEYER)

E iho ana o luna, E piʻi ana o lalo,
E hui nā moku, E kū ana ka paia.

There is so much
that cannot be said in English.
Cannot be seen in English.
Cannot be heard in English.
Cannot be mastered by English.

It is a whole shimmering universe.
And it is
alive.

Under the noise
of this one.

Under the well-beaten chest
of this loud and proud world
shouting its commands to everyone,
speaking on our behalf.

But this world,
the one they think
they made with their own bare hands,
with their single-male-god-creator,
made-in-their-own-image.

This world,
we are witnessing its
self-destructive end.

Its fossil-fuelled ambition
changing the climate itself.

It is out of ideas.
It is out of time.
It is over.

So much information
and on the brink of collapse.

It is in
our mother tongues
almost lost to us –
we will return
to the memory of wholeness.

Because
we have
different
things
to say
about being here
and being human.

In the Pacific, where I come from,
the largest ocean in the world
and the smallest islands.
In seventy languages
the word for placenta
is the same as the word for land.

Fonua, fanua, enua, whenua, honua.
To honour
that time you spent
in the drum of her
beating body.

When she was
earth, sea, sky to you,
the air that you breathed.
Fonua, fanua, enua, whenua, honua

We were ever aware of our
umbilical
dependence
upon earth.

Afterbirth,
planted with a tree, naturally.
Our fate
intertwined.

My placenta went up in smoke
in a hospital furnace.

A whole generation was lost like this:
ashes to ashes, dust to dust,
before we even began.

Let us stand.
Replant our feet
Connect.
Ground.
Sole to soul,
skin to skin,
to everything that guided us
sustainably
for centuries.

It is in our own past
that we will find our way back
to the future.

Word by word,
ancestors return,
speaking with terrestrial tongues
to hold up the sky.

What is above be lowered,
what is below will rise.
The islands will unite
and we will stand
and be strengthened.

Let all the islands of the world unite
with ancient song, poetry and prayer,
with rituals of love for our Mother
and practices of care.
Let us listen again to the languages
of ocean, earth and air,
so we can understand
her plans
for a return
to balance.
Translate,
narrate,
create
a future
we can all
live in.

Let us remember ourselves back
into elders,
worthy of generations to come.

E iho ana o luna, E piʻi ana o lalo,
E hui nā moku, E kū ana ka paia.

MATARIKI: A CALL TO KĀINGA

Kāinga, 'aiga, 'āina.
Let the morning mist
remind us
with its cold, fresh breath,
that we are alive.

Matariki:
marked by a constellation high in the sky,
barely visible to the human eye,
known to collectives of seekers
searching for signs,
lashing ancient
markers
of time.

Can we return to rhythm?
Remember lives lived along the arc of a
    wiser calendar?
When we were allowed to wax and wane
with life itself?

Matariki, can we stop?
Our fossil-fuelled forever forward,
full speed towards an irreversible end?

Can we take stock?
One million species endangered.
The ruin of rivers, fallen forests
the mined, the fracked,
a carbon-choked sky
holding his breath
for us.

We are a water world.
Oh ocean, we ask too much of you.
Gagged, plastic-bagged.
You hold too much heat
on our behalf.
Vast dead-zones
oxygen-deprived,
acidic tides.

Missing and murdered
beneath your waves.
Coral reef graves
point their bleached,
broken fingers at us.

No, tomorrow
is where we find ourselves
today.

Heads or tails?

If ever the world needed to come
full circle
it is now.

                                      Matariki,
                                      time to honour different ways
                                      of seeing the same night sky.
                                      Different ways of being human
                                      and being alive.

                                      Let lost languages
                                      give us ears so we may hear,
                                      eyes so we may see.
                                      Hearts so we can translate
                                      the thudding rhythm
                                      of the co-created:
                                      that which feeds us, breathes us,
                                      the substance under our feet,
                                      fresh water that flows in our veins,
                                      air in our lungs,
                                      stardust in our bones.

                                      Let us call on our family of relatives
                                          to help us heal.
                                      Bright light of the stars,
                                      fierce power of the tides,
                                      enduring knowing of the stones,
                                      cleansing of water that can still heal
                                      everything it touches.

Then let us attune
beyond sound
to that most profound
to mauri/mauli –
the essence.
So we can stand in sacred places
that have plans for us
encoded into the soil of its soul.

Build the marae/malae
to house a future we can live in.

Let us not just build meeting houses,
let us be meeting houses,
let our bodies
house the meeting
that needs to happen.
For we are out of time.

Mataliki, Matariki, Makaliʻi, Mataʻiki
Time to stop. To take stock.
Pause and reflect on all that we've lost.
To remember our dead. To shed.

End the aching arc of bitter farewell.
Find fresh.
Enter a new cycle,
following hard-earned,
hard-learned bends
of where we have been before.

Awaken.
Act.
Hope for another
turning turn.

THE
ART OF

WALKING IN DARK LIGHT

TE KOREKORE

In the beginning there was nothing.

Open expanse,
space without place,
a vast void,
empty abyss,
endless.

Absent
of all form,
eternally open
to every
possibility.

In its emptiness
lay its fullness.

The void in which
nothing was felt.

The void in which
nothing was in union.

In its nothingness
lay the source of
every something.

The void in which
nothing was possessed.

Precondition
of every probability.

Precursor
of all promise.

TE PŌ: THE DARK AGES

The dark
in which nothing
was seen.

The long night,
the dark night,
the deep night,
the great night,
the intensely black night.
Long, expectant,
deeply gestational
black upon black.
Heavily pregnant,
an amniotic night
awoke
a night of feeling.

From the night of feeling
came the restless night
of tossing
and turning.
From the
restlessness
emerged
the groping,
from the groping
the reaching,
from the reaching
the seeking,
from seeking
returned following.
Twinned, paired,
pushed, pulled,
repulsed, attracted –
finally union.

From union,
conception:
the birth
of everything
we know.

TE AO MĀRAMA: THE WORLD OF LIGHT

From conception
began the swelling.
The swelling gave rise
to energy.

From energy
emerged
deeply
subconscious.
Eventually,
subconscious
evolved into
mindfulness.

From mindfulness
rose longing.
Longing begot
desire.

From desire
and longing
came forth learning.
Learning led
to theorizing.
From theories
evolved shape
and form.

Appearance
Appeared,
which gave rise
to discernment
and sense.

Sensing
stirred grasping,
grasping
gave us possession,
possession
enabled
being equipped –
which aroused
the wielding
of power.
Power:
the authority
to exercise
will.

From all of this awareness
we entered
the world
of light.

UNBECOMING

That once smooth,
running flow of will
confuses its current,
doubling back on itself
in doubt.
All of the anticipated
chain reactions
and actions
edge away
from one another –
uncouple
unhinge.

What was once automatic
has slowed,
the machinations
slightly irregular –
out of order.

Dread
that what was once
is irrelevant,
instead.

Disoriented,
disempowered,
your taste for possession
and your hunger
to occupy your
place in the world
diminishes.

Empty-handed,
Unequipped,
footing unsteady,
you lose your grasp
on almost
everything
slippery
to the touch.

You sense
that even your
sense
of sense
is suspect.

Suspicion quickens
into silver panic,
lightning quick
and damaging.

One
melting moment
after another.

Anxiety attacks
of hot, quicksilver flash.

When forms and shape
morph and whir,
twist and shift
into unreliable

appearances
and disappearances,
you know
you are right
on the edges
of the world of light.

Familiar faces
contort, reflecting
features belonging
somewhere
you don't recognise –
somewhere where
you're not supposed to be.

Everything
betrays you.

Tricky and twisting.
Theories spiral out
lavishly
back in on themselves –
double over,
a criss-crossed crisis.
You are unlearning
everything you thought
you knew.

Desiring nothing,
losing longing itself.
Lost to yourself.

Mindfulness,
elusive, rare,
perhaps
best avoided.

Subconscious centre stage,
dreamlike in an opera dress,
lip-synching to voices
no one else can hear.

Even she
removes her lipstick,
exhausted,
leaves the room.

Contracting,
collapsing,
deflating –
a dangerous kind of thinning,
like a ring become so thin
with wear
in the wind
it begins to whine
in a way
that makes it sound
like something alive:
open mouthed
and in pain.

Elemental energy is
drained,
the underside of
the laws of physics
bent, broken, not bothering,
repelling, disconnecting,
undoing, uncoupling,
bonding nowhere.
It's lost its charge –
disintegration,
disunion.

There is no following
and there is no seeking.
There is no movement at all.
Nothing to grope for,
nothing to hope for.

You let go.

Stay still for so long
the edges of your hours
and cusps of your daylight –
shades and shadows –
blurs, darkens into dusk.

You are foetal
when you first enter
the realm of the night.

You push past
evenings of
tossing and turning.
Sleepless and open-eyed,
you move past the night
where there was still feeling
until it's gone, gone, gone.
You move into
where nothing is seen.
You stay there so long
you lose your eyes.

Without eyes, without insight,
you drop effortlessly into the dark night.
You spend so much time in the dark of the
   dark night,
it becomes the intense night.

You sink so low in the intense night,
you find yourself deep in the deep night.
So much time passes in the deep night,
it evolves into the long night.
The long night stretches so far beyond long,
it can only be called the great night.
And then, you slip past
the last of the night doors.

Pass beyond
the realm of night itself
and enter the abyss.
This is the realm of nothingness,
where all boundaries collapse.

The void where nothing is in union.
The void where nothing connects.
The void where things barely touch.
The void where nothing is felt.
The chasm in which nothing is possessed.
The void of absolute nothingness.

Few come back from this place.

THE ART OF WALKING IN DARK LIGHT

If you can pass

through the dark doors
of the nights,
fall through their lonely
sequences of
intensity,
lack of colour
and depth,
you will eventually
lose faith in daylight.

Nothing will ever
appear to be
what it once
seemed
again.

If you can let night,
shadow, light
press hard
down on your body,
void it.
Find yourself
lost
there.

If you are
brave enough
to pass through
and do not take death
into your own hands,
but still give up
on everything
you thought you were,
and let all that you believed
become dead to you,
know you will lose
almost everything
that meant anything to you.

It will be
the breaking
of your own
understanding.
You will lose
faith
in
faith
itself.

To survive it
you must become
empty and as open
as the expansive void
you occupy,
so bare
there is no longer anything there
but the free-floating dust
of ideas
about who
you once were.

No longer felt.
No longer possessed.
No longer in union.
The emptiness of it
annihilating.

Yet in your emptiness
lies your fullness.

From your formlessness
emerges all possible shape.

In your openness
lies every branched-out,
forked and twigged-tipped ending.

The purity
of nothing.
Release.
Relief
from beliefs.

A clean slate
of complete
combustion.
A demolition,
an erasure
of all
the thin, narrow,
impossibly
premeditated
pathways
you let yourself
live by –
lost to you.

The end
of an identity
under strain.

Only the blank-slated body
can free itself
completely
for a
completely
new story

of self,
in a world
forever
altered.

Unbecoming.
Becoming.

Death.
Life.

Being
Un-being.

More than can
be imagined
in-between.

GODDESS MUSCLE MEDITATION

In her soft open arms,
she gathers all the parts of me:
spinning thoughts,
whirring anxieties,
memory shards,
fear fragments,
pieces lost in
floating rumination.

She brings all of this
lost and found,
splintered, split,
back to me –
in golden arms,
carries it to my core –
she encourages me to

breathe
myself home –

into my heart;
the only
part of me
that can bear it,
that can break.
And break
again.

Awake with more knowing,
e x p a n d i n g.

She draws me deep
into my own dark
embodied –
beyond the
stretched-skin
of soft flesh,
to what's
within.

I know
that slippery slope,
thalamus to amygdala,
spiking blood sugar,
spinning medulla,
serotonin signalling,
the hijack, erratic,
hormonal, heretic,
the rushing adrenal –
so often numbed,
dopamine doped,
and dumbed.

She brings me
back to myself:
down my
deep-down-slide
to the organs inside –
where my sick
knowing
resides –
all the
indigestible
of going against
my own knowing.

Those dark, resting
hiding places,

where it all   stops
                            clots
                            blocks
                            stagnates
                            sick

the
thick
viscous of
slow moving
sweetened condensed,

the acidic
biting back:
acetic, acerbic,

the desperate
balancing acts
of alkaline:
trying to figure shit out
on behalf
of all that is natural
in my body.

The leftovers in my liver –
trying, for bile.

It is the blood star
of my cervix
that shakes
her bloody
red head.

No more.

Co-dependent
co-morbidities.
Pre-dispositioned
precancerous.

She pulls me past
self-sabotage
towards the
muscular organ
beating so badly
at the
heart
of me.

Takes me
to my centre.

She says – *stay
here.*

Breathe.

She points to my heart.

Chambers
I have neglected.

I enter.

Breathe.

I find myself
alone
with my
self –
centred.

A room of one's own.

Breathe.

Now, she says,
Stay.

*Hold yourself gently,
for you are gathered
together for a reason.*

She reaches
for the far flung,
        the deep-in-night
parts of me
        that only the
dream birds –
        god-messengers –
can carry.

The hurt and harmed,
too hard for me to hold
in the light
without fracture.

I feel her pull
for the pieces of me
being held by others.
Not for safekeeping,
but bound tight,
in hot heavy hands,
held in spite –
stuck in freeze and flight –
wound around sentences
where I am held tight –
buried and storied
as failure.

She retrieves,
relieved,
and says

Breathe.

I press
my own mess
to my chest.

Blame, shame,
broken, betrayed,
the humiliated
and abandoned.

Although I do not want to –
I hold it
        to
                my
                      heart.

My resistance stands
on dark sandbars
of deadlands, wastelands,
landscapes of lost lovers,
defeated friendships
old battlefields.
I see one empty black beach
that I cannot step
    a
        foot
              on.

Feke writhe
in those thrashing waters.
Where stands dread.
Tentacles clinging.
Bruised interlocked strangle
of entanglement –
the underwater of it –
the barely breathing ...
Reminiscent of
eldest enemies.

Breathe.

She says.

Hold it all gently, for they
were gathered around you
for a reason

Even as I shudder,
I hold it closer
to me
than ever before –

in this room of my own –
dark, damp chamber –
beating wildly.

We hold it all
with gravitas:
the deathly,
the destroying
the dangerous.
We feel it all.

She calls on
rain, rain, rain.
Saline and salt,
aqueous and mucus,
secretion, excretion,
the surging overflow
releasing, relieving
parasympathetic
undertow.

We cry.

The flood, the deluge, the stopbanks breaking,
The too much, the rush, the unstoppable gush,
She holds it all in her unconditional arms.

She touches the tides with moonlit hands,
She pulls all the world's water.
The fresh, the saline, the salty, the sweet.

She runs a river through me –
the fast flush of flow –
the slow moving elixir
of murmuring movement. Shift.

And then the ever-undulating of ocean. Adrift.
This deep dive, beyond the depths
of my shallow breaths.
A salty galaxy dark
as outer space.
The pregnant pulsing of spawning sea.
Lifegiving since time began. Free.

I watch her, our Mother,
harvesting wind and wave, stone and stream,
light horizon and deep trench in outstretched
 arms,
she heats and hums, she sings and spins,
she pulls the stars down into the deep
into the world's darkest water:
Lit.

She pulls this liquid magic
into the adulterated body
that has carried me, child,
through all I have known.

My excess, my distress,
my ruined and wrecked,
the dream-lives that died
at my own hands.
The withered bloom
of true love, with its broken branches.
The wilted wanting,
                          the waste.

It is
a fertilising,
     forgiving flow
          of star light
               fresh and seawater
poured
into the hurt, harmed
damaged and dead:
the decomposing.

It is a forgiving fertilising flow:

Blood streaming refreshed,
cleansing astringent,
dissolving, dismantling,
not washing the unwanted away –
but keeping it all
in her fecund, fertile arms.

This rich real mix –
of mud, blood and bone.
Where heirloom seeds are finally
birthed
and grown,
in the soil
they have been
sown for.

Much-longed-for
embryos –
unfold,
acts of daring –
reaching for leaf-like life

trusting
they will thrive
in conditions
we have all been waiting for:

the unconditional.

These long-hoped-for seedlings
reach out into the arms of forests
of upstanding ancestors –
dreaming themselves alive –
through these kernels,
now unfurling,
uncurling,
into their own
nature.

we breathe.

The endlessly regenerative of it,
as she tends to all of us,
equally.

Everything, I have ever felt and ever known
is a part of her already.

All of it
in her orbit.

Every beach, every bone,
every taniwha set in stone,
every grain of dark grief, it is all held
by her beautiful body.

Everything is home.

She holds
even my dead grandmother
in her universe,
alive, in the slow-moving glide
of turtle. She can be found

in the sharp of my shark;
the whiplash of stingray;
the wide wingspan of two birds of prey:
kāhu and kārearea;
in the hula of the ʻiwa birds;
Hiʻiaka's beautiful ones.

She is the guide
in all of our guardians.
Each kaitiaki
entrusted with
returning us
home.

In the dark night life-changing
visit of ruru.
In the protective shape of Rupe, Lupe,
holding a sacred covenant
between its wings.
In the miracle flight
of the tavake –
able to come back
from beyond
the beyond –
te korekore –
te pō,
return
re-formed.

She is everything known
and unseen:
everything
in-between.

Every woman
I have ever loved,
makes herself
in her own image.

She is
the full circle
of the centre.

Finally,
I feel her
breathing
in my
own.

I *breathe* it all in,
unconditionally,
via venous channel, to the core –
and *breathe* it out arterial routes
expanding to *breathe* in more,

to enliven all that I am –
a blood vessel
rowing my ancestors ashore.

All of us tributaries
in the return
to source.

ACKNOWLEDGEMENTS

This poetry book is dedicated to my mentor, te reo teacher and dearest friend, Papa Sean Bennett-Ogden (22 November 1964–26 July 2019). Kua hinga te tōtara i te wao nui a Tāne. You taught me so much and gave me the language to describe another world. Ka aroha.

To Dawn Patchett, my step-mother, who also left us (29 March 1937–15 January 2020). Thank you for helping me find my voice and forever believing in me. I adore you.

To my children, Karlos, Nikolas and Maka Toa, who gift me grumpily to the universe and then take me back again. Thanks for understanding that Mum is a writer, poet and real person in the world who needs time and space to be creative. You are my three little walking worlds. I am so proud of who you are. 'Ofa lahi atu.

Many thanks to all my nameless beloveds who accompanied me in various ways, at various stages, along my journey. So many of you will find yourselves in here. I love you.

To all the readers, fellow writers, librarians, school teachers, lecturers and students, the independent bookshops and organisations such as the Commonwealth Foundation that have made me feel like my voice is worthy of being heard, and have created a Pasifika lit community ready to receive my words – thank you! I am grateful and humbled. Aroʻa atu.

To all the artists who contributed to the book: Meleanna Meyer and the team of artists who created the mural that appears in this book 'Aloha 'Āina – thank you for your kōkua. To Naomi Maraea who painted the incarnation of Hikuleʻo, tēna koe. You know how much it means to me and my Nana. We are grateful for your eyes that see. To Delicia Sampero, I know I have all the words, but there are never enough words for your images. Thank you, I am profoundly moved by how seriously you took this task and how deeply you felt into it. Danke schön.

To Kanikani te Manakura who helped edit this volume of poetry and gifted me the title. I am indebted. To the fluent tongues of the Moana, my friends and willing translators, Sefita Haoʻuli of Tonga, Dr ʻEmalani Case of Hawaiʻi, Dr Ramona Tiatia and Jaslyn T Mariner-Leota of Samoa, Papa ʻOta Tuaʻeu and Maʻara Maeva of the Cook Islands: mālō, māhalo, faʻafetai lava, meitaki.

And finally, to Huia Publishers, Eboni, Te Kani and the team of editors, designers and marketers who made *Goddess Muscle* possible. We did it! I'm really grateful.

I wish to acknowledge Creative New Zealand, Fulbright New Zealand and the Mental Health Foundation for grants that enabled this poetry book to be written. To have enough money to clear time for creativity is bliss. Aloha kākou!

Lastly, Nana – Alice Suisana Hunt-O'Keefe – you'll always be the biggest fan of my work and my greatest supporter. I'm sorry it took me so long to publish this one. Rest in peace, Nana. Love you always. Alofa tele.